Betrayal

Copyright © 2015 by William Crotty

All rights reserved. No part of this book may be reproduced without the express permission of the author's representative or publisher.

Published by The Piscataqua Press
An imprint of Riverrun Bookstore
142 Fleet Street | Portsmouth, NH | 03801
www.riverrunbookstore.com
www.piscataquapress.com

Printed in the United States of America

ISBN: 978-1-939739-71-1

About the Author

Robert Crotty (1937-2013) was a student of the human nature he wrote about. He received a MFA in English from the Iowa Writers' Workshop during the Raymond Carver/Kurt Vonnegut years. He also attended the graduate journalism program at the University of Missouri at Columbia. At one point he was a reporter and editor of a Maine newspaper. There were other positions: professor, dean of a college and director of the American Civil Liberties Union of Maine among them. He wrote mostly from Kennebunkport where he and his family lived and later from Portsmouth, New Hampshire where he worked for a time and acted in stage plays. Bob was a forceful and gifted writer. He came from a large and loving family. Bob and his wife Mary Jane Burbank had three sons, Sean, Liam and Brendan. He left behind in addition to his writing many happy memories.

See also: http://www.liamcrotty.com/american-literature-the-teacher-by-robert-crotty/

Betrayal

a screenplay by

Robert Crotty

FADE IN

Two Continental Army non-commissioned officers are fishing in Lake Champlain, a sergeant reading directives and a corporal diving for fish. Northwest a solitary Mohawk Indian runs through woods to the base of Sugarloaf Hill. Ten miles north two women with red shawls dance in the rear of General John Burgoyne's British army.

PROLOGUE ROLLS over: gold-helmeted Hessians carrying huge packs.

British Redcoats jostling each other and singing as they march.

Two German bands play spiritedly.

Wagons filled with colorful sets creak along.

Ahead of the slowly-moving 15-mile column, two teams of horses pulling cannon plunge past Mohawk and Tory advance scouts.

Betrayal

PROLOGUE

In the summer of 1777 King George the Third and his military advisors agree on a strategy of dividing and conquering the rebellious American colonies.

INSERT which SHOWS map of New York State

Bringing 9,000 troops under General John Burgoyne south from Canada to capture Fort Ticonderoga on Lake Champlain is the first step.

Sending a few thousand Mohawk Indians, Tories, and British regulars under Barry St. Leger to seize Fort Stanwix in the Mohawk Valley is the second step.

Transporting thousands of crack troops from Sir William Howe's main British army in New York City [north on the Hudson River] to rendezvous at Albany will be the third step.

The combined forces will surround and destroy the rebels' northern army.

This will isolate New England -- the hotbed of rebellion -from the rest of the colonies and strangle the rebellion.

In late July of 1777 Burgoyne's army slowly wends its way south, sharing his certainty that the rebels -- "those country clowns" -- will run away, Fort Ticonderoga and Fort Stanwix will fall, and the flames of revolution will die before the first snow falls.

A Screenplay

                                    CUT TO:

EXT. LAKE CHAMPLAIN BY FORT TICONDEROGA DAY

SERGEANT BRENDAN SULLIVAN in a rowboat
reads directives from General George
Washington on gambling and General Horatio
Gates on fishing.

CORPORAL ELIJAH PIGGOTT dives with a
sharpened twig to spear fish, surfaces,
comments, dives again. They are playing a
leisurely game of cards.

                    SULLIVAN
          'The Commander-in-Chief
          expressly forbids all officers
          and soldiers playing at cards,
          dice, or at any games except
          those of exercise or diversion',
          etcetera etcetera, 'baneful
          vice...destructive influence'
          .What's he about, Corporal
          Piggott? Our George Washington
          loves a good wine, a frolicky
          dance with the ladies, and a
          friendly game of cards. What's
          this mush? Feed my soldier son
          rotten pork, shoot off his leg,
          send him home with smallpox for
          the family, but do not -- no
          never -- expose my darling boy
          to the evils of gaming!?!

                    PIGGOTT
          General Washington's trying to
          polish Quaker apples.
                    (Dives.)

Betrayal

                    SULLIVAN
          Quakers? They won't fight. On
          either side.

Sullivan moves to the other side of the
boat.

Piggott surfaces and discards two cards and
takes two others.

                    SULLIVAN
          No, they hide their fat sons in
          the buttery when recruiting
          officers call. Spout their
          religious beliefs--Holy
          Pacifists for Profit.

                    PIGGOTT
          Quakers don't approve of gaming
          but they have great cheeses and
          sides of bacon. Root cellars
          full of turnips and onions and
          squashes in the winter. Tubs
          full of hard coin -- not our
          squishy Continental paper money.
          General Washington will take all
          what he can get. Gin. Fish ho!

Piggott lays down his cards and dives.

                                   MOVE TO:

INT. FORT TICONDEROGA HEADQUARTERS ROOM -
DAY

American GENERALS HORATIO GATES and JAMES
ST. CLAIR examine coins and maps and
discuss Burgoyne's strategy.

A Screenplay

LIEUTENANT RICHARD VARICK paces nearby. In the background Gates's two aides sip tea, casually unpack several bags, and whisper.

>   GATES
> Where is he? I have to believe that Johnny Burgoyne has been held up in Canada. Or might he (pointing to map) choose to bypass our little welcoming committee here at Ticonderoga? No. He is impulsive and self-indulgent but not a fool. He would not leave his supply line exposed.
>
>   ST. CLAIR
> Did you not serve with Burgoyne, General Gates?
>
>   GATES
> Burgoyne and I served in the Home Guard in London but were not intimates. I did, nevertheless, attend one of the theatricals that he penned and David Garrick presented at the Drury Lane Theatre.
>
>   ST. CLAIR
> What is your considered opinion of him?
>
>   GATES
> A middling good playwright.

Betrayal

ST. CLAIR
I meant, how do you esteem General Burgoyne as a military man?

GATES
A middling good playwright. (Both laugh.) Forgive me, General St. Clair, I understood you perfectly. John Burgoyne is shrewd, ambitious, and loyal to his own vision of himself as a great man. And he is, truly, a particular friend of the King. Yes, he loves theatricals, but—

VARICK
In Boston the British staged one of his plays and the Patriots called him Swagger Burgoyne.

ST. CLAIR
That's most instructive, Lieutenant Varick.

GATES
-- but any Patriot general who thinks he faces a foolish London fop--(Leans toward map.) It would not be a bad strategy to pretend to bypass you via Lake George, feint toward Albany, then swing back to -- yes, Varick. Are you dancing or do you have an urgent need to be excused?

A Screenplay

                VARICK
General Arnold's scouts believe
that a force of Indians and
British and Tories seen on the
St. Lawrence will come from the
West to Fort Stanwix. General
Schuyler believes (Gates gives
St. Clair a knowing look) they
will try to recruit Tory militia
before joining Burgoyne and Howe
near Albany.

                ST. CLAIR
Thank you for the lesson in
strategics, Lieutenant Varick,
but General Gates brought that
information with him. We just
might be able to sip this
exquisite tea from India and
peruse my collection of coins
without your constant
attentions. Have you packed your
effects? Lieutenant Varick
completes his most recent three-
month enlistment tomorrow.

                GATES
This must be near ninety years
old, Sinclair, struck to
commemorate General Monck's
refutation of Oliver Cromwell
and return to his first true
allegiance to the monarchy and
to Parl -

                VARICK
I never understood why Moncks
was treated as a hero. Did he
not turn traitor to Cromwell and

the Puritans? How could
Parliament and the King trust
that he would not --

              ST. CLAIR
Lieutenant Varick, you are the
interruptingest -

Gates raises his hand to stop St. Clair.

              GATES
Moncks was a traitor to Cromwell
but a hero to supporters of the
Monarchy. In short, Mister
Varick, General Moncks chose the
right side -- the ultimately
victorious one -- at precisely
the right moment. Homeward bound
tomorrow, eh. Been fully packed
for three weeks? Uh -- fetch
Sergeant Sullivan to me, Varick.
Most likely he is to be found on
the parade ground, drilling the
militia. (Varick smiles as he
leaves.) A handsome coin,
Sinclair, even if the subject is
a shade dubious. (Lowers his
voice.) I appreciate your
keeping Young Varick on your
staff these three months,
Sinclair.

              ST. CLAIR
Despite his lack of manners and
his incessant curiosity, Varick
could add value to your staff.
He reads every military manual,
works tirelessly, respects
Continentals and militia, and

A Screenplay

writes a clear, forceful prose.
But you heard him quote his two
heroes, Arnold and Schuyler.
Arnold he worships from afar.
His old mentor Schuyler he
writes to frequently. (almost
daily)

              GATES
Since Congress set Philip
Schuyler and me a not-so-merry
game of musical chairs with this
northern command, I almost feel
a kinship with him.

             ST. CLAIR
I must admit to having felt much
more confidence in our cause
when you commanded us last year.
One hopes that Congress will see
the proper light this season.
They toast each other with
raised teacups.

EXT. MOUNT DEFIANCE DAY

Mohawk warrior captain PRINCIPAL is
pointing out Fort Ticonderoga on the banks
of Lake Champlain to British COLONEL
WILLIAM PHILLIPS.

PRINCIPAL Far Phillips.

             PHILLIPS
General Phillips, if you please.
Not too far for these long guns.
In fact a perfect distance,
(Looks over his shoulder) if a

trifle steep. Good work,
Principal.

> PRINCIPAL
> Capn Principal if you please.

MOVE TO:

EXT. HALFWAY UP SUGARLOAF HILL DAY

An exhausted British artillery squad led by SERGEANT GARFIELD BURBANK is resting against trees where ropes are being used to pull a second long gun up to Mount Defiance. THE YOUNG PRIVATE begins to slide down a tree toward the ground.

> BURBANK
> Don't sit, Son. Don't sprawl. You'll never get up. That's it, Men, just lean for a moment. The savage told General Phillips that only a goat could climb this hill and your intrepid Phillips said, 'Where a goat can go—"

Waves at soldiers who chime in.

> SOLDIERS
> "'--a British Redcoat can go.'"

> BURBANK
> "'And where a Redcoat can go--'"

> SOLDIERS
> "'He can drag a cannon after.'"

A Screenplay

> BURBANK
> All right, Men, we'll put her in place and drop a few balls on the rebels. Keep them amused until General Burgoyne comes up in a day or two and then we'll give them what for. we'll sweat out last night's rum. Up and at 'em. (Groans from men.) Thank God and King George that I am only with you temporarily. This much regular pleasure could kill a man. Up, down, and up we go, Lads. Bring that rope 'round.

CUT TO:

EXT. LAKE CHAMPLAIN DAY

Sullivan, close to shore, is reading a directive, mostly to himself. Piggott is alternating between rinsing pages in the lake, lining them up on drying racks on shore, and cleaning fish.

> SULLIVAN
> And now Good Corporal Piggott we have Granny Gates's directive against 'dilatory fishing'. (Reads to himself.) Hmmm. Could he have wind of our little scheme selling the smoked fish. No, he's not talking about us, Corporal Piggott. We know the manual of arms by heart. Can't a man fish and learn how to kill at the same time?

Varick comes to the edge of the water and calls.

Betrayal

> VARICK
> Sergeant Sullivan! General Gates wants you. Now!

> SULLIVAN
> You can tell Granny Gates to hold his water, Young Varick. (Holds up fish.) We have engaged in serious, not dilatory, fishing. (Rows to shore, stern first.) What does it feel like to be a short-timer?

> VARICK
> I feel as if I'm leaving a garden half grown, but then the weeds are choking -what is that strange corporal doing?

Sullivan dons his fancy fringed leather hunting shirt and briefly affects a British accent.

> SULLIVAN
> Corporal Piggott, is it? He's rinsing his legal briefs. Did you know, Piggott is suing the King of England for alienation of his American subjects' affection.

> VARICK
> How do you put up with him?

> SULLIVAN
> Put up with him! He's the best corporal I've ever had -- on either side of the ocean.

A Screenplay

>   SULLIVAN
> A trifle eccentric. (Slight
> pause.) All right, he's passing
> strange.

Varick and Sullivan watch Piggott cleaning fish and throwing them in a pile on the shore. He goes back to sorting pages.

Piggott's dog Old Lump contentedly suns himself on the shore.

>   SULLIVAN (O.S.)
> All right! You've persuaded me!
> He's rollicking mad! In dark old
> England, he would be locked up
> forever in Bedlam! But here, in
> this country of madmen who think
> they breathe new air, who think
> to challenge the world's finest
> army, who claim new gods and the
> privileges reserved heretofore
> for nobility, Corporal Elijah
> Piggott fits nicely in. He
> seems, in fact, quite ordinary.
> (Pause.) Rather mainstream tame.
> (Pause.) Terribly, terribly
> dull. (Calling.) Corporal
> Piggott! We must needs instruct
> Generals Gates and Sinclair.
> Carry on smartly.

Mock salute from Sullivan.

Piggott gives elaborate salute, drops page in water, dives after it.

Varick turns away, shaking his head.

INT. FORT TICONDEROGA HEADQUARTERS ROOM DAY
St. Clair is refilling Gates' teacup.

> GATES
> At least Philip Schuyler couches his occasional observations as suggestions. Benedict Arnold will weary you to death with his demands straight from Jehovah's mouth.

> ST. CLAIR
> Exactly! I must fortify Mount Defiance. I must teach flanking to militia. I must have two or three old hulks ready to sink in the lake and block –

> GATES
> Block Burgoyne who sails this way on ships captured at Valcour Island from Arnold. He loves to be hailed as the hero who sent the British back to Canada last season but Arnold is less fond of reminders that he lost our entire fleet in the bargain.

Varick enters, salutes; followed closely by Sullivan who mimics his walk.

> VARICK
> General Gates, I have Sergeant Brendan Sullivan outside. Shall I bring him in?

> GATES
> (Hides smile.) Do -- yes, do that, Lieutenant Varick.

A Screenplay

> VARICK
> (Calls as he wheels about.)
> Sergeant Sullivan, front and --
> oop!

> SULLIVAN
> Is that -- that 'oop' -- a
> mannerism left over from
> studying the Mohawk Valley
> militia? Sir?

Gates and St. Clair are laughing.

> GATES
> Enough, Sullivan. Are the men
> ready?

> SULLIVAN
> As ready as this lot of farm
> hands and shop boys will ever
> be, Your Grace. They will be
> honored by your visit this week.
> They read your directives with
> the keenest of interest,
> Excellency. Just now a soldier
> broke his fishing pole and asked
> for more marching drill.

Varick grimaces.

> GATES
> Splendid -- if only passing
> true. Now truly, Sergeant, how
> do the troops from the various
> colonies tolerate each other?

> SULLIVAN
> The New York State Militia and
> the New Hampshire State Militia

-- the word 'colony' is enough to start a tussle, Your Eminence -- those two argue ownership of the Hampshire Grants, what is newly called Vermont.

               VARICK
They concur only in disparaging Massachusetts men as 'Lousy Levellers' because they dress as plain as Old Sam Adams and think like him that no man should rise too high above another in this new nation.

              SULLIVAN
Then they all unite to resist commands of Corporal Piggott and myself.

                GATES
Insubordination? Mutiny!

              SULLIVAN
No, Your Grace, rest easy. I heard Baron Von Steuben explain it to our good General Washington. When drilling Prussian soldiers, Von Steuben told them what to do and they did it. When he drills our American militia, he tells them what to do and they wait for him to explain why it is most beneficial to do it that certain way. Then they do it...usually ... unless they have questions. He was not used to persuading soldiers to their duty.

A Screenplay

>   ST. CLAIR
> Nor,- I imagine, to soldiers who
> take pride in wearing fringed
> hunting shirts.
>
>   GATES
> We used to give five hundred, a
> thousand lashes to any soldier
> who showed disrespect when I
> served in His Majesty's Army-
>
>   VARICK
> They still do. Colonel Daniel
> Morgan is ready to show his
> scars to any shrinking militia
> man.
>
>   SULLIVAN
> A mere 499 lashes. But that form
> of enlightened discipline will
> not wash here. Thirty or forty
> lashes is considered severe by
> our militia who think that God
> has chosen them to weigh each
> word that sounds suspiciously
> like a direct order.
>
>   GATES
> When I served in His Majesty's
> Army-
>
>   SULLIVAN
> Did you not once mention, Your
> Excellency, that you rose
> through the ranks, were actually
> a humble lowly sergeant in his
> Majesty's army like myself?

Betrayal

> GATES
> I must have told you that story, Sullivan. My mother a scrubwoman. My good fortune in having Sir Horace Walpole as my godfather. Where is your memory, Man? It was a stroke of luck, Sinclair, that brought my mother to...

Sullivan steers Varick to the sideboard where a decanter of sherry and glasses sit.

> SULLIVAN
> Memory tells me this will give us ample time to test the sherry. A glass, Young Varick?

> VARICK
> Don't call me -- that's General St. Clair's private stock. what gives you the right -

Sullivan raises his glass to silently toast Gates' officer aides who turn away.

> SULLIVAN
> Aren't they a friendly lot.

Sullivan empties his sherry glass.

> VARICK
> They're probably shy in new surroundings.

> SULLIVAN
> Shy about picking your pocket face to face. You couldn't tell a shying away from a deliberate

snub if your own horse walked by with his nose in the air -Sir!

                    GATES
...Thus, Sinclair, in a short time my merit and my good fortune raised me to a rank, before I left for these shores, far above that which George Washington begged the King for some ten years running. (Lowers his voice.) Certain members of Congress have asked me to Philadelphia to discuss -- to keep them informed of -- is this the time to add to one's staff a talkative young zealot -- I truly admire Varick's fealty to Schuyler, but certain -- uh -- military secrets in the hands of a radical like Old Sam Adams could prove -- perhaps if Varick stayed in his Mohawk Valley -

                   ST. CLAIR
He has indicated that that may be his intent. I detect a certain dissatisfaction, perhaps ennui with his military service to date. If we can not furnish him with a stately white horse, suitably caparisoned, and a sparkling sword to lead glorious cavalry charges-- A cannon ball crashes through the roof, breaking the teapot and cups, scattering saucers, spoons, milk and sugar.

Betrayal

GATES
My God!

Sullivan races outside.

Varick watches Gates's aides fuss over him to see if he is wounded.

Sinclair scoops up his coins and runs to the doorway.

ST. CLAIR
How could they reach us with their little six-pound popguns...?

SULLIVAN
(Calling O.S.) They're on Mount Defiance. with the long guns. (Re-entering.) British artillery squad. And a Mohawk

VARICK
(Crossing to Gates) Sir, what orders?

GATES
Uh -- ahh -- General St. Clair -- in charge here. He will order - give orders. Congress expects me - to Philadelphia. I must ride -- to my men -to Philadelphia. Carry on, St. Clair.

ST. CLAIR
You do not wish to assume command here, General Gates?

A Screenplay

>   (Chases after Gates who is
>   stuffing tea and sundries into
>   his bag.) Sir?

                              CUT TO:

EXT. PARADE GROUND - DAY

Piggott is dragging a huge ornate trunk past deserted cooking fires, stopping to sample a turkey which he confiscates.

As he reaches the racks where his legal papers are drying and fish cooking, he calls to men who are running in all directions;

>   PIGGOTT
>   Two for one! Fresh fish and
>   sweet turkey! Today only! A
>   little food for your trip!

Piggott examines each legal paper -- scanning, selecting, discarding, laying down, picking up again -- before tucking each and every one in his trunk as men throw paper money and coins at him and grab fish and tear off chunks of turkey.

                              MOVE TO:

INT./EXT. HEADQUARTERS ROOM/PARADE GROUND - DAY

Gates runs outside, trailing documents on the ground which his aides scoop up.

Betrayal

                GATES
Ho the gate! Bring me my horse -
- any fast horse! NOW! Whatever
you decide, St. Clair, my full
support. Duty lies with my army
to the south. I'll go them in
this hour of peril -- directly I
finish my business with
Congress. God speed!

              ST. CLAIR
Thank you for -- the excellent
tea. (To Varick.) Assemble the
officers in headquarters room.
You will meet with the sergeants
in the bombproof. We will
prepare an orderly retreat with
smudge pots and fires.

               VARICK
Sir! We have three months'
provisions. Retreat!?!

              ST. CLAIR
Shall we pit your eighteen
months of tent service against
my nine years on battlefields
... if we act smartly,
Lieutenant, our three thousand
will live to fight another day.

                                  MOVE TO:

EXT. ENTRANCE TO BOMBPROOF DAY

Varick watches short, dumpy Gates trying to
mount a frightened horse as his aides pile
bag after bag on pack horses.

A Screenplay

Sullivan and a few of several dozen sergeants are holding candles in the dark shallow bombproof.

A cannon ball lands near the mouth of the bombproof.

All stir uneasily waiting for Varick to resume speaking.

> VARICK
> (Head lowered, mumbling.) Tell your men then to take only muskets, water bottles, two days' food. Leave all else. If—

> SULLIVAN
> Begging the lieutenant's pardon, Sir! Could you speak up please! And shall we take axes?

> VARICK
> Yes, Sergeant, thank you. Muskets and axes and two days' provisions! If we keep our heads --

Varick turns to see Gates riding furiously out the main gate, ignoring St. Clair's farewell and Gates's aides who each struggle with the reins of three heavily laden pack horses.

> VARICK
> -- and travel light, we will all survive this. The main body of Redcoats and Hessians may be two days' march north, but watch for Indians and Tories in the

Betrayal

advance... our scouts have not returned.

MOVE TO:

EXT. BANKS OF LAKE CHAMPLAIN - EARLY MORNING

Montage. American militia and Continental troops fleeing down both banks of Lake Champlain.

Fort Ticonderoga in the near background is still full of smoke used to conceal last night's retreat.

Work parties harvesting crops.

Sullivan throwing bags and chests, including Piggott's ornate chest of legal documents, out of overloaded wagons.

Some bags open to reveal candleabra, bolts of cloth, chrystal, china, and silverware.

Two soldiers drop back to retrieve loot.

One uses candleabra to bribe his way aboard a wagon.

The other drags his huge bag behind him; fails to hitch a ride and falls back.

He is stunned by a Tory hatchet and scalped immediately by a Mohawk.

EXT. REBEL CAMP WITHOUT FIRES - NIGHT
Sullivan is packing his saddlebags.
Soldiers huddle for warmth.

A Screenplay

> VARICK
> Where do you presume to be going?

> SULLIVAN
> I have decided that I might flourish more under General Gates's command to the south than in these cold and hostile northern climes.

> VARICK
> (draws pistol) You will help us or I'll shoot you for a deserting dog.

> SULLIVAN
> Three dispatches, Lieutenant Varick. General Philip Schuyler informs General Arthur St. Clair that he is sending 200 woodsmen to slow Burgoyne's advance.

EXT. SOUTHERN SHORE OF LAKE CHAMPLAIN - NIGHT

Two hundred tall, lean woodsmen are double-timing northwards on the road beside the western bank of Lake Champlain.

They carry huge axes.

Young boys carrying torches run ahead and beside them.

> SULLIVAN (V.O.)
> Felling trees, tearing up bridges and corduroy roads, driving cattle and sheep into

the deep woods, and burning crops. He suggests we do the same as we retreat.

RETURN TO SCENE

              SULLIVAN
Or as General Schuyler says, in his arch way, 'advance southward.' The second dispatch is from General Benedict Arnold ordering me to Philadelphia to assist him before the Pennsylvania Council. The third from General Schuyler to you.

Varick tears the dispatch open.

              VARICK
General Schuyler wants me to testify at his Congressional court martial. Is all government gone mad! Burgoyne marches south, St. Leger threatens the Mohawk Valley, Howe looks to turn north and we shall all be explaining to politicians in Philadelphia why the war effort is not effectual. I shall not miss this weak madness.

              SULLIVAN
Perhaps we can cheer Congress with news of how well our southerly advance goes here in the northern department.

Varick lowers his pistol.

A Screenplay

                    VARICK
Someday your little jokes will
get you killed.

                    SULLIVAN
An ending devoutly to be wished
for. My father on his deathbed
was telling a racy jest to my
mother with his hand on –

                    VARICK
If I raised this loaded pistol
to your brain, would it end your
ceaseless chatter?

                    SULLIVAN
Loaded, aimed, and fired might
give you a few moments' peace.
But then -- the eulogy --
Lieutenant Varick, Sir, I leave
you Corporal Elijah Piggott to
cover your -- uh -- withdrawal.

                    VARICK
You're leaving me to trust one
strange man to cover our
retreat, Sergeant Sullivan?

                    SULLIVAN
You are the only officer, Young
Varick, other than Benedict
Arnold who has ever thanked me
in public. (Mounts.) Please
consider a re-enlistment.

                    VARICK
I seem to be preoccupied with
other matters, Sergeant, and
stop calling me 'Young Varick'.

I am near twenty-five years old.
Where is he?

            SULLIVAN
Piggott's back there -- God pity
the Tory scouts and even the
Savages -- furious with me for
heaving his trunk of legal
papers and for not taking him to
Philadelphia. He plans to
research there a suit against
our good General Washington for
charging exorbitant expenses to
the young republic.

            VARICK
You're leaving me to trust one
truly mad man with --!

            SULLIVAN
Piggott on the skirmish is worth
a regiment.

EXT. WOODS - DAY

Piggott finishes setting a snare.

He fires a rifle from the crook of a tree.

Piggott races to another tree where a rifle is waiting and shoots the Tory scout who discovers the first rifle.

            SULLIVAN (V.O.)
As you hear single shots,
Piggott's still using his
rifles. When you hear two
muskets fire together, it will
be time to move your men --

A Screenplay

rather rapidly. Lot's wife obtains.

RETURN TO SCENE Sullivan mounts.

          SULLIVAN
Au 'voir, mon ami, Le Jeune Vareek. Just practicing, Lieutenant, in case the Frenchies do decide to come in on our side. God speed your journey to Philadelphia.

          VARICK
(Mumbling.) Should I decide to come. (Turns away and calls.) Two muskets is the signal, Men! Have torches ready.

EXT, INDEPENDENCE HALL - MORNING

GENERAL PHILIP SCHUYLER in a velvet coat and silk shirt with ruffles and Lieutenant Richard Varick in dress uniform alight from a fancy coach and hurry up the steps to Independence Hall which houses the impressive Pennsylvania Council's chambers on the first floor and the United States Congress's cramped meeting room on the second floor.

Schuyler, jumping two steps at a time, pauses to wait for Varick.

          SCHUYLER
I much prefer, Richard, to not be late for my own Congressional court martial since I requested it and since I know for a

certitude that friends of
Horatio Gates would be happy to
crucify me in absentia.
Varick catches up and they
proceed with Schuyler in the
lead.

VARICK
Might we stop, General Schuyler,
for half a moment to see how
General Arnold's hearing before
the Pennsylvania Council
progresses. In the spring of my
year at Yale I watched him drill
his militia on the New Haven
green, and I wrote him a hundred
times last year in preparing the
Valcour Island fleet, but I've
never even talked to him. He
seems to accomplish what others
won't even hazard. If he had
been at Ticonderoga-

SCHUYLER
St. Clair made the right
decision. One only hopes
Congress sees it in that light.
Arnold speaks highly of the work
you did in procuring supplies
and shipbuilders for Valcour.
And you have made an arduous
journey on my behalf. Don't fret
about Johnny Burgoyne. We've
slowed his army from five easy
miles per day to one torturous
one. He's fully engaged with
that and his ripe young
mistress. A glimpse it is.

A Screenplay

MOVE TO:

INT. PENNSYLVANIA COUNCIL CHAMBER DAY

GENERAL BENEDICT ARNOLD is pacing back and forth, up and down, reciting his grievances to a skeptical JOSEPH REED, chairman of the Pennsylvania Council, eleven Councilors, and interested onlookers such as JOHN ADAMS and WILLIAM HAZEN.

Poring over documents at the small defense table are MAJOR DAVID FRANKS, Arnold's chief aide, and Sergeant Sullivan.

>   ARNOLD
> ...if my reputation, my service to my country at Boston, Quebec, Valcour, Danbury is to be negated and disparaged, my proud family name to be impugned -- my ancestors' honor was handed down to me unsullied. Is it now to be trampled by mendacious men seeking preferment by character assassination...

>   REED
> (Loud whisper to Hazen) Proud family name -- his father was a sot -

>   JOHN ADAMS
> (leaning forward) And his great grandfather was governor of Rhode Island, successor to Roger Williams.

Schuyler and Varick enter, stand in back.

Betrayal

REED
General Arnold, we are met as the Pennsylvania Supreme Executive Council to require of the fifth Benedict Arnold, not his esteemed ancestors, why we should not pursue charges that he -- that you -- did knowingly issue illegal passes to a privateering vessel The Charming Nancy resulting in enormous profits to you and your suspected Tory co-owners; that you did use government wagons to transport private goods, again for obscene private profit; that you misused miitary personnel -

ARNOLD
(Aside to Franks and Sullivan) There's what's stuck in his craw! I sent Reed's son for a barber. The poor dear. As far as his fighting prowess on the battlefield goes, he should be—

REED
-- that you assigned veteran military personnel to duties not befitting their experience or rank -

ARNOLD
-- sent for seamstresses; he could advise on pretty little dancing uniforms.

Sullivan snorts, covers his mouth.

A Screenplay

Franks blushes, tries to restrain a silly laugh which escapes him.

>   REED
> (Enraged) Does General Arnold think these proceedings arranged for his amusement!

>   ARNOLD
> General Arnold begins to think these proceedings were designed to puff up the importance of little men with big appetites for power and place and international acclaim. General Arnold respects His Grace General Washington and field generals such as Greene and Schuyler, but has no use for—

>   SCHUYLER
> (To Varick) He includes me as a compliment, but others will think—

>   REED
> General Arnold, you will not refer to anyone in this government, in our army, in these entire United American States as 'His Grace.' We do not hold with monarchies or kingly titles. Is that clear, Arnold.

>   ARNOLD
> It is becoming chrystal clear to General Benedict Arnold that you have brought him here to insult him -- me and the military

Betrayal

offices I hold. I am too proud
of the brave officers and men I
have led from New Haven to
Boston, through the Maine
wilderness to Canada, up and
down Lake Champlain -- many of
them gone to their eternal rest,
unable to defend their heroic
actions -- to have their
nobility sullied by a pack of -

JOHN ADAMS
(Rising) General Arnold! Please!
Do not say or do anything that
can not be undone. Even those of
us who admire your exploits must
ask that you, like General
Washington and all military
officers, account for your
actions.

REED
And your financial transactions.

JOHN ADAMS
This fragile union we are
forging has civilian purview of
the military -- we must needs
ask our most renowned fighting
general for -- please tell The
Council what you wrote in your
spring letter.

REED
Arnold corresponding with John
Adams. Who'd have thought -

ARNOLD
My spring letter?

A Screenplay

Sullivan thumbs quickly through a pile of papers and hands a letter to Franks which he reads to Arnold.

>FRANKS
>'Dear Friend Adams, A coterie of desperate men, a cabal of jealous.

Schuyler taps Varick lightly on the shoulder as Arnold pauses to scan the letter.

Varick strains to hear every last syllable as they leave.

>ARNOLD
>Conscious of the rectitude of my intentions, conscious of my duty to truth and honor, (Schuyler pulls Varick through the doorway) it must be said -- I pointed out to Mister John Adams -- that all thirteen of these spurious charges were lodged against me by the same few doubtful men who have formed a desperate coterie, a jealous cabal. One sits there at the right hand of Mister Reed --a certain William Hazen whom I court martialed for insubordination at Quebec. Since then he has waged a cowardly private war against me to -

>HAZEN
>(Jumping to his feet and reaching inside his vest) You --

you bloody strut of a bantam
rooster! I disagreed with you in
open council and you treated me
as enemy! I'll see you dead!

Council members restrain Hazen from raising
his pistol as the lovely Peggy Shippen
enters with a plain-looking female friend,
draws Arnold's attention. Men make room for
them in the front row. She sits, leans
forward eagerly.

              ARNOLD
(To Hazen) Not meet me on the
field of honor! Hide behind
committees and cabals -- (Aside
to Franks and Sullivan) My God!
Who is that creature! Franks,
she's gorgeous. I must send her
a note.

              FRANKS
That is Peggy Shippen, youngest
daughter of Edward Shippen, a
quiet Philadelphia Quaker.

              SULLIVAN
Rumored to be a Tory.

              FRANKS
As for notes, I have here the
letter you sent to young Betsy
DeBlois in Boston. It was
returned with the trunk of
dresses you sent her. Obviously
not effectual.

A Screenplay

                ARNOLD
(Reading softly) 'Twenty times have I taken up my pen and as often has my trembling hand refused to obey the dictates of my heart... hmmm. A union of hearts... callous to every tender sentiment if the taper of love is not lighted up at the flame'... yes, this will do nicely, Franks. Change, of course, any necessary particulars.

                FRANKS
The General would not consider a stout Patriot wench rather than these brittle Tory bird-girls?

                ARNOLD
Let Washington have his plump widow. I much prefer...

Just as people are settling down and Hazen is escorted out, a DISPATCH RIDER rushes in and hands a message pouch to Reed.

                REED
General Arnold, this takes precedence. (Arnold goes to Reed.) Some 2,000 of the enemy under Barry St, Leger and Chief Joseph Brandt have come to Oswego via the St. Lawrence and Ontario lakes and are pushing for Fort Stanwix. Washington has immediate need of your services in the northern department. You are excused. This hearing stands

adjourned. If you wish, Arnold, I will convey this upstairs to Congress. Washington stressed the urgency—

ARNOLD
No thank you, Mister Reed. General Washington's confidence in me is most gratifying despite attempts -- General Arnold shall take it upstairs to Congress himself. (Wheels about.)

Reed stands and talks loudly and then shouts at Arnold's back.

REED
I served as Washington's secretary and as adjutant general. If I choose to call -- these hearings will reconvene! We will find out once and for all if -

ARNOLD
I am as certain sure of it as that your brilliant letters from the battlefields of America will live forever. The adjutant general does not interpret maps? On mine the St. Lawrence is still a river. As John Burgoyne might say, 'Ta!'

MOVE TO:

INT. CONGRESSIONAL MEETING ROOM - DAY

A Screenplay

Varick on the witness stand in the cramped, crowded second story room is being questioned by JOHN HANCOCK, presiding officer in the Congressional court martial of General Philip Schuyler.

SAMUEL ADAMS sits just behind and a little to the left of Hancock, occasionally passing a note.

Schuyler sits upright and alone at the shaky, battered defense table.

          HANCOCK
A crucial question, Lieutenant Varick, in assigning responsibility for the abandonment of Fort Ticonderoga without the firing of a single shot is: did General Schuyler ever address the fortification of Mount Defiance?

          VARICK
(Softly.) General Schuyler on visits to Fort Ticonderoga twice recommended that Mount Defiance be fortified.

          HANCOCK
Recommended but did not order. Why?

          VARICK
That, Chairman Hancock, is General Schuyler's style of command; he prefers to persuade. I must admit to accepting the prevailing wisdom that we did

not need to fortify because of the steepness of the hill. I was wrong. (Audience buzzes.) I believe, however, that had we a small detachment there, they might not now have scalps and the same results or worse obtain.

HANCOCK
You do not return to duty with the northern Continental Army?

VARICK
No, Sir. I believe my duty presently lies at the home of the McCreas, my foster family, in the Mohawk Valley. Tories, Regulars, and upwards of 1,000 Mohawks under Chief Joseph Brandt are rumored to be en route. I have served six three-month enlistments and my intended and I –

HANCOCK
Thank you, Young -- Lieutenant Varick.(Samuel Adams passes a note.) I have been provided one further question to ask you: Are you or will you be working in General Schuyler's campaign to be elected governor of New York State? Or might you be active in General Gates's campaign to be elected to the New York State Assembly?

A Screenplay

>   VARICK
>   Wh -- what! N -- no, Sir. I had
>   no idea that such a campaign --
>   campaigns -- was even -- were
>   even contemplated.

Varick looks at Schuyler who is shaking
hands with John Adams; at Gates who is
whispering to Joseph Reed as he enters from
the rear stairway.

>   HANCOCK
>   (O.S.) Thank you, Young Sir.

Arnold marches in, diverting attention. He
is followed by Franks and Sullivan and a
group of young officers.

>   HANCOCK
>   Straightforward answers from a
>   military man seem to be the
>   exception, not the rule, in this
>   building. On behalf of the court
>   -

>   ARNOLD
>   Begging your pardon -

>   HANCOCK
>   -- I wish to express -

>   ARNOLD
>   A spot of trouble up north,
>   Commander Hancock -

>   HANCOCK
>   -- our gratitude and our hopes
>   that you will return to us soon.
>   The Continental Army needs more

officers such as -- we are not
yet ready to commence, General
Arnold, proceedings in the court
martial you have so earnestly
and repeatedly requested.

          ARNOLD
I beg to interrupt, Your
Worship. A little -

          HANCOCK
I do not employ the title
'Commander' and I am not 'Your
Worship,' General Arnold, here
or anywhere else. We are forging
a republic where each man is -

          ARNOLD
A little emergency up north,
Your Hon -pardon me -- Mis --
ter Han -- cock. A little
difficulty requiring my
attention... (hands dispatch to
Hancock) according to... uhh
...His Excellency?... General
Washington that is.

          HANCOCK
(Frowns at Arnold, reads.) This
certainly takes precedence -

Arnold takes the dispatch out of Hancock's
hand and turns to rejoin Franks and
Sullivan and the young officers.

          HANCOCK
No one has ever disputed your
brilliance in the field, General
Arnold, but your attitude in

other areas of our common
endeavor leaves –

                 ARNOLD
All in good time, Mister
Hancock. In the interim,
Congress can endeavor commonly
to repay me for my Quebec and
Valcour Island expenses and
resolve the delay of my
promotion to major general and
proper seniority. Should you
need to contact me, look for the
red -- British Redcoats and
their officers' blood -- and
there will you find Benedict
Arnold -- the Fifth.

Varick leaves the witness chair to rejoin
Schuyler. They go to the lobby as Arnold is
surrounded by his young admirers.

January 8, 1998

                 VARICK
How can Congress be so mean-
spirited? Why don't they pay the
expenses owed General Arnold and
promote him to the rank he has
earned ten times over!

                 SCHUYLER
A long story, Richard, best told
short. Perhaps because Arnold
has demanded his due. He will
not flatter this conceited
Congress which poses for world
adulation. Perhaps because
Arnold rarely misses a chance to

rub salt in a wound, par example, addressing Hancock as 'Commander', the same Hancock who dreamed of leading the Continental Army before Washington was selected. Schuyler scans the lobby, nods and bows as he talks.

SCHUYLER
Perhaps also -- no, definitely -- because Congress dreads a strong-minded man on horseback. Standing armies dominating civilian government.

VARICK
But General Arnold is our best fighting general by far -- the only one the British and Indians fear.

SCHUYLER
Yes, fine to keep a fierce dog on a leash in the front yard, but in the drawing room he can upset domestic plans. And Benedict Arnold is not an easy man: respects no one but Washington and men who take up arms. He despises the French, par autre example –

Schuyler nods to Gates who is also scanning the lobby while talking to John Adams and Samuel Adams.

A Screenplay

                    SCHUYLER
          General Gates is remarkably
          active. John and Samuel Adams.
          Cousins but rare bedfellows.
          John wouldn't invite Sam to tea
          under threat of death. Now
          Horatio Gates brings them
          together hand in glove.

Schuyler turns back to Varick who has been
watching Sullivan receive an envelope from
Joseph Reed.

Benedict Arnold enters the lobby from the
hearing room talking loudly to young
officers. Franks is trying to get him to
lower his voice.

                    ARNOLD
          Canada! If they sent me a
          thousand healthy reinforcements,
          Canada would now be our
          fourteenth state. But no! These
          aspiring demigods sent Benjamin
          Franklin and his committee of
          three to ask me if I had not
          promised too much to Natanis,
          the Abenaki who saved us from
          starvation. A thousand pounds to
          rescue an army in foreign
          territory. 'What was your
          authority, General Arnold?' I
          should have hanged all three
          and—

                    FRANKS
          Please, General Arnold, please.

Betrayal

ARNOLD
Why should I not make an honest profit from The Charming Nancy? Do we ask Commander Hancock how his uncle smuggled the family into respectability! Does General Washington account for the contents of wagons he sends south to Mount Vernon each month? These petty indoor politicians while natural men in the field risk all -- (Watches Peggy bend, glance, smile) look at that creature! We must, Franks, communicate with that wisp of loveliness before we answer our summons north. Goodbye Gentlemen, for now, but please not au 'voir.

Arnold shakes hands with the young officers.

SCHUYLER
(V.O.)-- despises Benjamin Franklin who dances now with the delicate ladies of the French court. Congress, naturally, is not fond of Arnold's opinions, a bit embarrassing as we try to woo France into this war. And Arnold is too open-minded for the mean-spirited and the vengeful, too entrepreneurial and ostentatious for the Levellers, too flexible for the conservatives. He does not readily distinguish between Patriot and Tory when it comes

to men who have earned financial
prominence -- nor to young
ladies with obvious charms.

                VARICK
    Is it true, General Schuyler,
    that you are seeking the
    governorship of New York and
    General Gates is a candidate
    for—

                SCHUYLER
    My best regards to your family,
    Lieutenant Varick. Safe home.

                VARICK
    Thank you, General. I only ask
    to—

Schuyler abruptly leaves to join Gates and
John and Samuel Adams.

                GATES
    ...He means well, but the same
    could be said of St. Clair or
    most generals. Obviously, Mount
    Defiance should have been
    fortified. A direct command from
    Schuyler rather than an arch
    suggestion would have ensured
    it. Still, the plain men of New
    Hampshire will not serve
    cheerfully under a land baron
    with thousands of New York
    acres, a hunger for Vermont,
    fancy clothes, liveried servants
    -- ah, General Schuyler, we were
    just discussing –

Betrayal

                SCHUYLER
    I'm sure you were.

Varick tries to intercept Arnold who is en route to Peggy Shippen.

                VARICK
    General Arnold, I am Richard
    Var—

                ARNOLD
    Yes, yes, so good to see you
    again. Miss Shippen, may I say
    that you are more excruciatingly
    beautiful than even the most
    exalted reports.

                PEGGY
    General Arnold, I thought you a
    hard man of thunder and
    lightning bolts.
    I did not know you had soft
    words to turn a young girl's
    fancy.

                ARNOLD
    Would that I had words to
    describe loveliness that
    transcends all...

Varick watches momentarily as Gates and Schuyler and Arnold continue their campaigns.

Sullivan steps behind Varick.

A Screenplay

                SULLIVAN
   May the road rise with you,
   Richard Varick, and God hold you
   in the palm od His –

Sullivan sees Samuel Adams disengaging from his circle and moves toward him.

                VARICK
   Thank you, Sergeant Sullivan.
   (nods, gives mock salute) What
   shall I do without your...
   attitudes to color my day. Safe
   home. You seem to know Mister
   Reed quite well?

                SULLIVAN
   (calling back) I am home.
   Wherever there's a warm dispute,
   Tom Paine and Brendan Sullivan
   are -- safe home to you. When
   you grow weary of the rustical
   life—

Sullivan turnns away, catches up to Samuel Adams.

                VARICK
   I shan't -- I doubt that I
   shall. My intended and a well-
   regulated -- a better life await
   me. When we drive the Tories and
   the Mohawks out of the Valley, I
   expect to lead a quiet -- I
   shall not miss –

Sullivan whispers to Samuel Adams. Receives small purse. Varick looks around. All are engaged but he leaves.

Betrayal

FADE IN EXT. MCCREA FARM IN THE MOHAWK VALLEY DAY

HON YOST is juggling.

JANE MCCREA tries to imitate him, fails, drops a stuffed sock, frowns.

Principal watches Jane intently.

His Oneida companion SECOND RUNNER is listening to the preacher SIMON KIRKLAND and watching Principal watching Jane.

Principal looks into the shards of sun glinting off Jane's blonde hair and SEES a fuzzy, fractured nude image of Jane trying to juggle.

Second Runner whispers sharply to the wide-eyed Principal.

>   SECOND RUNNER
>   She is not for you.

Startled, Principal cocks his head toward Second Runner, looks back quickly to see fully-clothed Jane chuckle as her three socks tumble to the ground.

>   SECOND RUNNER
>   She will mate with her own. You
>   have a good woman, my sister,
>   waiting for you in our
>   longhouse. She is not for you.
>   She never will be.

A Screenplay

Principal continues to stare at Jane who is bending to pick up her juggling socks.

Second Runner cuffs Principal playfully.

>   SECOND RUNNER
> Besides, you smell like a man of the Iroquois and you are as old as the mountain.

When Principal does not react immediately, Second Runner leans toward him and whispers fiercely.

>   SECOND RUNNER
> She calls you savage! She comes to claim the lands we live on as her own. She comes to take the food from your son's mou—

Principal shoots out his arm to grab Second Runner by the throat.

>   PRINCIPAL
> I am not old.

>   SECOND RUNNER
> Uhh -- all right. (Principal releases chokehold.) But you are a Captain of the Mohawk married to a Princess of the Oneida nation. we are of the Six Nations of the Iroquois. She is not for you.

                                    MOVE TO:

EXT. TRAIL LEADING TO MCCREA FARM - DAY

Betrayal

CAPTAIN JOSEPH McCREA and Richard Varick ride toward the McCrea farm arguing politics. Joseph wears a red British officer's coat with a white cloth around his arm. He carries a white flag. Varick wears his dark blue Continental dress uniform.

                  JOSEPH
I will admit that your little hero Benedict Arnold has inclinations to act the role of gentleman: he signed a pass through the lines for me immediately on hearing that you are my foster brother. How did you get him to dance your tune, Richard?

                  VARICK
I have just met him for the first time in Philadelphia and it was not satisfactory. But General Arnold respects work I did last summer in sending materials for the fleet he sailed to Valcour Island.

                  JOSEPH
That glorious victory at Valcour, yes?

                  VARICK
In a way. Your fleet won, but ran back to Canada for repairs. Arnold lost our fleet but gained us a year's time to—

A Screenplay

                    JOSEPH
        To what? Prepare your sorry
        troops to abandon Fort
        Ticonderoga whthout firing a
        single shot when Johnny Burgoyne
        showed up.

Varick swallows and turns red.

                    VARICK
        Prepare our new country to
        struggle to victory. Burgoyne
        shall never reach Albany.

                    JOSEPH
        Richard! You are spinning with
        the stars again. He is but forty
        miles north of Albany with
        Phillip Skene and thousands of
        Loyalists ready to join his
        march. How on earth do you—

As they round a bend, Varick spots Jane.

                    VARICK
        Jenny!

Jane turns, sees Principal watching her, and then sees Joseph and Varick.

                    JANE
        Joseph! Welcome home!... Varick.
Jane laughs as socks tumble on her head and shoulders. She hugs and kisses Joseph and pecks Varick on the cheek.

BURT TIMMONS takes the reins of both horses and shakes hands with Joseph.

Betrayal

> VARICK
> That is my welcome after three months away? Your juggling session with the half-wit is more important? Why is Hon Yost here?

> JANE
> If you think I should be perpetually panting hot for your arrival, think again. Try leading with your head one time -- (leans and whispers) and not your arrogant cock.

> VARICK
> Jane! I saved myself for you.

> JANE
> Why? I remember requiring nothing of the kind. Feel free to share.

> VARICK
> Jane! We're all but formally engaged!

> JANE
> All but formally. (She looks at her bare ring finger) Isn't that a brilliant arrangement. We must needs talk, Varick, but Mother's been holding Sunday dinner for you and Joseph—

Burt holds Joseph's reins as he takes small packages from his saddlebags. Jane turns and gooses Joseph who acts shocked.

A Screenplay

               JANE
-- that dandyish brother of
mine.

               VARICK
Come to the belfry before
service, Jenny.

               JANE
I'll come to the belfry -- and
talk.

               VARICK
Is that my bother of a brother
Burt, or half a brother, talking
to the horses?

               BURT
It -- it is. Welcome home,
Richard. I -I mih -- miss -

               VARICK
I missed you too Burt. But I am
home now. To help you rebuild
our farm.

               JANE
Oh God, Richard, you've
forgotten the ass end of a duck
from a cow. You are not quite
Thomas Jefferson Philosopher-
Farmer. Burton, talk to your
half-baked half-brother --
should he allow you a word
edgewise!

Burt frowns as Jane spins and charges off.

Betrayal

Varick extends his hand. Burt steps forward and hugs him.

                    BURT
          I ha -- have sss -- summat to
          tell you.

                    VARICK
          I am through chasing this war. I
          am home. There will be plenty of
          time to talk. Something smells
          awfully good. Turkey! Put the
          horses away and I'll save you a
          seat the other side of Jane.

                    BURT
          I amm gg -- going ff -- for -

Varick hurries toward the house to catch up with Joseph and Jane and does not hear Burt.

                    VARICK
          There will be no Tory uprising
          in this valley...

INT. MCCREA HOUSE DAY

Reverend McCrea presides absent-mindedly at the dining room table laden with a huge turkey and vegetables and cranberry sauce and pickles and breads and cheeses and relishes.

The Reverend Simon Kirkland hurries in from outside, nods bashfully, and sits beside Jane just as Burt is about to sit there.

A Screenplay

Mrs. McCrae sits to her husband's right and reminds him with a gentle tap on his forearm that it is time to say grace.

                JOSEPH
You have 300,000 young men who could be in the field. How is it then, Dear Richard, that Washington flees Long Island with 12,000 patriots and can only muster 5,000 lonesome fools when he reaches New Jersey.

                BURT
There are many fuh -- farmers who must needs ah -- attend to -

                THOMAS
You're entirely correct Burt. There could be many reasons that -

                VARICK
Would you have us believe, Dear Joseph, that your paid assassins the Hessians are fighting a holy crusade to protect the freedoms of all Englishmen?

                REVEREND
Let us bow our heads and give thanks.

                JOSEPH
If you had the recruits, Richard, you would not -- sorry Father,

Betrayal

> REVEREND
> Thank you Gracious God for bringing us together to celebrate your goodness and bounty. Thank you for bringing our eldest son Joseph home under flag from service with General Howe in New York City. Thank you for bringing son Thomas safe home from his medical duties with General Washington and our foster son Richard back to our Valley to help Burt with their farm. Thank you for honoring us with this surprise visit from our esteemeed colleague Reverend Simon Kirkland. We see this sadness through different eyes; yet we both ask for Your Guidance. And thank you Dear God for keeping Jane and Mother and me healthy as we carry out Your Word. Thank you for this food which we will dedicate to –

As Thomas is easing a baked potato from the platter in front of him toward his plate, Mrs. McCrae taps her husband's arm.

> REVEREND
> -- to -- your greater glory.
> Amen.
>> THOMAS
>> Amen!

Thomas spears the baked potato and reaches for an ear of corn.

A Screenplay

                    ALL
    Amen.

Mrs. McCrea tries to keep the platters
circulating and encourages all to eat.

Joseph and Varick punctuate their
disagreements by thrusting the platters at
each other, ignoring everyone else.

Thomas, Simon Kirkland, Jane and Burt look
for an opening to try to participate in the
two-sided conversation.

Reverend McCrae cautiously studies the huge
turkey.

                    JOSEPH
          Had you the men you would
          neither clothe nor feed them.
          Deserters pour into New York
          with tales of starving men not
          half a day's march from the fat
          farms of Jersey.

                    THOMAS
          It is true our men have suffered
          terribly. Firecake and foul
          water is the dinner staple.
          weakness and disease kill more –

                    BURT
          Sh –– should the farmers be
          expected t -to give away their –

                    VARICK
          Must the Home Guard stay in
          England to protect Mad Old

Betrayal

George, leaving savages to do your dirty work!

          SIMON KIRKLAND
They are God's children and many are coming to Christ and the independence side.

          VARICK
But three years ago you fought beside me to chase off the drunken Mohawks who killed Mother and burned our farm.

          JANE
Many more are staying loyal to their benevolent father King George.

          VARICK
Have you now joined the Six Nations? Did the sachems name you He-Who-Hires-OthersTo-Spill-Blood?

          JOSEPH
I'll spill your blood, you tax-dodging Rebel.

Joseph and Richard get up and start around the table.

          VARICK
Come ahead, you Royal Toady!

They are careful to not bump the table as they rush to assume wrestling crouches.

A Screenplay

                MRS. MCCREA
Don't tear your coats! Father.
Stop them!

Reverend McCrae has been studying approaches to slicing the turkey. He is startled from his task.

                REVEREND
What? Stop -- stop that! Stop or I'll -I'll horsewhip you both!

Jane smiles at her father's familiar threat. Burt rises and begins to back out.

                BURT
I muh must go to the ff -- farm and... check -

                JANE
Stay, Burton. Maybe we could all go behind the barn, Father, and watch Varick and Joseph beat each other senseless? Just to give them a little holiday from the war.

Varick and Joseph stand straight and glance away.

                REVEREND
What did you say, Jenny?

                THOMAS
We are all family here. Must we air our differences now?

Betrayal

                    BURT
          I sh -- should -- tend the hh -
          horses

                    MRS. MCCREA
          Bite your tongue, Miss Saucy
          Mouth. I could use lots of help
          in the pantry.

                    JANE
          Carry on, My Darlings. Sit down,
          Burton. God grant your brother
          and mine are all bluff and
          feathers.

                                        CUT TO:

EXT. WOODS NEAR BURGOYNE'S CAMP DAY
Liveried, bewigged servants set an
elaborate long table for two.

In the background teamsters are driving
carts full of brightly painted sections of
stage sets into a circle.

A short, dour-looking youth ARTHUR
HUNNICUTT alternately scratches his wig and
pants and spins plates onto the table.

Chief butler WALTER BAILEY sees what Arthur
is up to.

                    WALTER
          Stop now! In London an army
          servant could be whipped daily
          for a week and tucked away with
          salt in his wounds. On the march
          we have no time for such

kindnesses. I have seen young
fools hung for chipping plate.

     ARTHUR
 Is it my choice 'tween that and
 washing, scrubbing, setting,
 clearing five times a day for a
 ham actor and his whore.

     WALTER
 (genuinely shocked) Arthur!
 Don't ever talk like -- look
 sharp!

Arthur turns to see GENERAL JOHN BURGOYNE
and his MISTRESS Approaching, hand in hand.

Following are Colonel Phillips who carries
several pieces of paper

Skene ignores Phillips throughout and
speaks only to Burgoyne.

     ARTHUR
 Oyy! It's David Garrick-Burgoyne
 and his tittiful mistress Lady
 Legsspread. Shall I set for a
 cozy three and we'll bring the
 whore's fat husband up from New
 York City in his new major's
 uniform.

Walter boxes Arthur's ears.

     SKENE
 It's important, General
 Burgoyne, that we issue any
 proclamations now to give our
 Loyalist friends assurance that

the Indians will be kept in
check.

                PHILLIPS
Can we assure General Burgoyne
that our Loyalist friends will
bring their own weapons and food
and not be a burden?

                SKENE
Most assuredly Your Excellency.
The Indian question and the
chance to catch a glimpse of
your magnificent army's might is
all that is keeping two thousand
well-provisioned Loyalists from
joining your march.

                PHILLIPS
General Burgoyne could sail his
troops down Lake George and be
in Albany in half the time.

                BURGOYNE
Arnold is on the loose somewhere
above Albany. Even if he has no
effectual force, his presence
will keep many from joining us.
If Barry St. Leger takes Fort
Stanwix easily -- and Arnold
gets no help from Washington...

                SKENE
When St. Leger takes Fort
Stanwix easily, Dear General.
The entire loyal contingent of
the Mohawk Valley will swell
your numbers to an irrestible

force. Arnold will be but a
fading memory.

               BURGOYNE
Mmmm. I should write to General
Howe. Tomorrow. First light.

               PHILLIPS
Your advice has nothing to do
with the miles of roads we build
through your property, does it
Mister Skene?

               SKENE
A mere matter of months Your
Excellency, -- if not weeks --
and the rebels will be crushed.

               MISTRESS
Johnny, it's lovely but is this
your idea of a little picnic --
excuse me Mister Skene but
Johnny -- General Burgoyne -had
this lovely-sounding idea about
getting away from his crushing
duties by returning to Nature.

               SKENE
Delightful idea Esteemed
Warrior. You may call me Major,
M'Dear. Nature is where you find
it.

Arthur finishes setting the elaborate table
and Walter checks it.

               MISTRESS
Won't you join us, Major Skene?

Betrayal

Burgoyne grimaces as Skene steps forward amd offers his arm.

As they walk a little way toward the carts of gaudy scenery which soldiers are unloading, Walter sets another place and Phillips touches Burgoyne's arm so they can talk quietly.

            PHILLIPS
That man is dangerous, Sir.

            BURGOYNE
Your prejudices do you little credit Phillips. We are dealing here with the woodsy country Loyalists who are decidedly a notch below their semi-educated brethren in New York and Boston. Woodsy yes. Dangerous? I rather think not.

            PHILLIPS
My aide called for his luggage yesterday.

Burgoyne shoots Phillips a glance of annoyance.

INT. SKENE'S PARLOR - DAY

A British officer followed by two Redcoats steps into the parlor and locates Skene's trunk and baggage.

As the two soldiers struggle with the trunk, the officer wanders to the other side of the room where something is on a board placed between two chairs.

A Screenplay

He pulls back and then approaches cautiously.

> PHILLIPS
> (V.O.) In Skene's parlor he found a dead woman on a board. Candles and clay and ice around her. A servant told my aide it is Skene's mother dead these three years. Mister -- Major Skene now enjoys a fifty-pound annuity paid to his mother every year she remains above ground.

BACK TO SCENE

> BURGOYNE
> Perhaps another strange colonial custom. I learned in Portugal that one needs make allowance for one's allies. Not to worry, Phillips. We will crush these northern rebels between us and Howe and St. Leger and then go for Washington. God willing, we will be back in London in time for the theatrical season.

Phillips and Burgoyne move closer to his mistress and Skene.

> MISTRESS
> Just to get away from that noisy camp with those -- dirty, smelly soldiers and their horrid women --

Betrayal

          PHILLIPS
For soldiers on the march, Madam, we require mainly that their muskets be kept clean. Not their breath, nor their songs -- nor the women who follow them.

          MISTRESS
Oh -- I am sorry Colonel Phillips. I meant no -

          BURGOYNE
Be a little easy with our friend, Phillips. She is not yet a veteran campaigner. (Holds seat for her and kisses her shoulder.) It's a bright new play, My Dear, the rage of London and our sets should reflect that light gaiety.

          SKENE
Exquisite. Just Darling.

Phillips tuns away as Burgoyne and Skene sit at the table.

          PHILLIPS
(softly) Not a veteran? By whose measurement?

          ARTHUR
Do they hang Colonels for chipping a whore's reputation? Speaking truth?

          WALTER
Serve the soup. With your mouth firmly shut.

A Screenplay

                    ARTHUR
And my eyes?

                                    CUT TO:

INT. MCCRAE KITCHEN - DAY

Jane carries a pie to the dining room.

Mrs. McCrae is taking puddings from the kitchen oven as Thomas stands by the pantry counter with potholders.

                    THOMAS
Why did you call us all home Mother? I had to tell my commander that father was ill.

                  MRS. MCCREA
He is. Or moving that way. Last week he secreted my sewing kit to the barn. I don't think he's sewn anything in thirty years. That's part of it, but I wanted us all to have this early Thanksgiving before the troops and savages take over the Valley and force us to bury our food and hide the stock.

                    THOMAS
Your cooking is wonderful Mother as usual. I wish the lads could taste-

                  MRS. MCCREA
I could send some turkey and trimmings back with -- oh... there are too many mouths.

Betrayal

Thomas smiles as he backs out the door to the dining room carrying a steaming pudding.

MATCH DISSOLVE TO:

Joseph is pacing from the kitchen to the pantry whacking his thigh with potholders.

                JOSEPH
Why are we all here, Mother?

              MRS. MCCREA
To see if anyone can solve your father. He sleeps and eats fitfully. Something is burning inside him but he will tell me nothing. 'Everything in its own time.' Two Sundays now he has given a sermon which no one understands, least of all he.

                JOSEPH
He may be worried about Mohawks heading toward Fort Stanwix with St. Leger. Split homes in the Valley could be subject to—

              MRS. MCCREA
No, no. This is how he is when he wrestles with a decision. Here, put one hot pudding by him but enough away that he doesn't burn himself.

Joseph starts toward the dining room but turns back.

A Screenplay

>JOSEPH
>Don't mention this to Richard, but the Brits treat Loyalist officers like draft animals. Though I bought my commission in the regular army, I am still a suspect colonial. My comments in council are clearly ignored. Sir William Howe's English staff decide not on military targets but where might be an amusing place to position oneself for the colder months.

Joseph pretends to dust his nose with a potholder as a handkerchief.

He flourishes a fork like a pointer, uses the calendar for a map, and affects an English accent.

>JOSEPH
>'Albany north and dark, Philadelphia south and bright. Not such a difficult decision.'

>MRS. MCCREA
>They are foreigners Joseph.

>JOSEPH
>We are all part of England, Mother, are we not?

>MRS. MCCREA
>To them the hind part.

MATCH DISSOLVE TO:

Betrayal

Varick brings an empty platter into the kitchen and stumbles. Mrs. McCrae catches him so he does not fall.

The platter crashes to the floor, bounces, and hits a corner of the stove.

              MRS. MCCREA
  Ohh!

Varick fidgets and eases toward the outside door.

              MRS. MCCREA
  That's all right, Richard. Thank you for trying to help.

Mrs. McCrae picks up the chunk of platter that has chipped off.

              VARICK
  Why are we all here, Mother McCrae?

              MRS. MCCREA
  Reverend McCrae is acting strangely. I thought together we might help him. And Burt is being more reclusive than usual. Perhaps both are struggling with a decision.

              VARICK
  I know I am. Once away from that weak and shiftless atmosphere of Continental Army life, I doubt I can return to it. I think I should prefer to wander around the Valley with General

Herkimer's poor farmer militia.
Don't mention this to Joseph. He
might –

    MRS. MCCREA
Will you and Jane take time to
talk? Or you and Burt?

    VARICK
Plenty of time for talking. I
just want to relax now and enjoy
being here. Right now I have an
urgency to answer Nature's call.

    MRS. MCCREA
As soon as you can might be the
best time

    VARICK
I'm on my way. Oh, you mean
talk. We will -- surely.

Varick rushes outside.

MATCH DISSOLVE TO:

Jane is tracing cuts on the crust of a pan of apple pan dowdy. She is daydreaming.

Mrs. McCrae impatiently waits for Jane to finish.

    MRS. MCCREA
What have you decided about Burt
and Richard? Will either of you
talk to him? Both? Don't let
things go on too long, Jane.

Betrayal

JANE
Thank you, Mother, for reminding me that I'm on the brink of spinsterhood.

MRS. MCCREA
I don't mean that, but you owe it to Richard to tell him what your mind is. He should at least know about you and Burt and Burt thinking to join Burgoyne.

VARICK
I don't know what I should say. Burton will never get the chance to tell anything. He'll be drowned under Varick's passionate speeches for a new order. I will tell him something before afternoon service. Is that why you called everyone home -- to force me to make up my mind.

MRS. MCCREA
Perhaps. And your father. And getting everyone together before the Valley is full of blood and bullets. But more... I've had an awful feeling that someone in the family is going to die horribly. I've had dreams but none have been clear. At first I thought it was Thomas. Then Joseph. I'm sure now that it's Richard. He has a genius for stumbling into harm's way. Do what you can to help me keep him here. I know he wants to stay.

A Screenplay

                    JANE
He is acting as foolish as ever.
He and Joseph have taken up
right where they left off --
barely have time to interrupt
their debating to eat. I will
always love a part of Richard
Varick but his passion for
upheaval scares me.

                MRS. MCCREA
I would rather a man dragged
indifferent cold to war than one
snorting in heat like a
stallion. The first will save
his fire for you; The other –

                    JANE
Burton seemed so tame to me for
so long. Almost cold. I thought
Richard was the man of passion.
But I see now that Burton feels
as deeply but does not force his
opinions on anyone. He seems the
sane and restful one now. And
Varick a noisy bag of wind. No,
that's not quite fair. I can't
decide anything.

                MRS. MCCREA
You will decide when the time is
ripe. Jane. I keep having this
dream, but I wake up in cold
sweats before I can see who it
is.

Betrayal

                    JANE
          Every mother in the Valley must
          be having those fears and
          dreams, Mother.

Jane and Mrs. McCrae carry the puddings
into the dining room where Joseph and
Varick continue to argue.

EXT. MCCREA BARNYARD - DAY

Hon Yost is recounting the beginnings of
the federation of The Six Nations to an
entranced Principal and a hungry Second
Runner.

All three have plates of turkey wings and
corn bread in front of them, but Second
Runner is the only one paying attention to
his food.

Hon Yost's eyes are almost closed and he is
swaying gently as he raises a handful of
twigs above his head...

                    HON YOST
          ...and the Great Peacemaker held
          the twigs and bound them
          together, saying, 'Strength
          comes with brother helping
          brother and tears follow the
          trail of brothers who fight each
          other. All here', and his hand
          reached out to the six tribes of
          the Iroquois, 'are brothers.'
          And the—

A Screenplay

> SECOND RUNNER
> There were only five tribes at that time. The Tuscaroora came later from the south.

Principal reacts as if he has been ripped out of a dream.

> PRINCIPAL
> Aaiyee! Whaaat!

Principal turns back to Hon Yost who momentarily looks lost and then tries to recover from the interruption.

> HON YOST
> -- the... five nations of the Iroquois lived in harmony and the Tuscaroora nation joined them in peace. No man alive remembers when any of the six nations fought each other nor their fathers nor grandfathers... until -

> SECOND RUNNER
> Preachers like Simon Kirkland opened the eyes of the Oneida and the Tuscaroora.

> HON YOST
> The Peacemaker appeared to me in the embers of last night's fire and said, 'I sorrow that the Six Great Nations of the Iroquois do not stand together. I see the blood of the Oneida spilled by the club of the Mohawk. I see the corn fields of the

Betrayal

>Tuscaroora burning from the
>torch of the Seneca. I see –

A pig oinks.

>SECOND RUNNER
>I see proud Iroquois warriors
>made to eat with the animals in
>the barnyard.

Principal lashes out at Second Runner who dodges nimbly.

>PRINCIPAL
>Be quiet when the holy man
>speaks or I will slice your
>tongue.

Hon Yost opens his eyes, fearful.

>SECOND RUNNER
>Perhaps I will return the favor
>first. After I slit the madman's
>belly and let all the words out
>at once.

>HON YOST
>Belly? (Shuts his eyes.) I see
>the bellies of the Six Nations
>slit open. I see strange
>headdresses on Mohawk chiefs and
>Oneida longhouses burning --
>fire and blood –

Terrified, Hon yost stands, still holding his plate of food, and hurries off moaning and keening.

A Screenplay

> PRINCIPAL
> When the holy man speaks you
> will listen.

Principal rises and follows Hon Yost. Second Runner calls after him.

> SECOND RUNNER
> I have heard these tales of the
> six great nations since I played
> child's games. There are only
> two sides now. If we do not go
> north to Canada we must kill for
> one or the other. Listen to your
> old squaw stories of The
> Peacemaker. I will sharpen my
> tomahawk.

Second Runner helps himself to Principal's food.

INT. MCCRAE DINING ROOM – DAY

Joseph and Varick are consumed with each other. Everyone else at the table is reduced to intercepting platters whenever they can.

Reverend McCrae is cautiously slicing small pieces of turkey.

> JOSEPH
> There are hundreds of people in
> the Valley loyal to King George
> but fearful of their radical
> neighbors who—

Betrayal

VARICK
Who have suffered at the hands of the Tory militia. Two Patriot barns burned past midnight—

BURT
Buh -- burning a man's beh--barn sh-- should be a hanging offense.

Thomas rescues a bowl of green beans from the Joseph-Varick exchange.

THOMAS
There have been cruelties on both sides. Have either of you read Doctor Samuel Johnson's "Taxation Is No Tyranny"? I hate to admit such, but he does reason—

JOSEPH
Brilliantly. There is no denying his argument.

VARICK
No denying he has sold his ability to reason for three hundred pounds annual of the King's money.

JANE
Admit it, Varick, Doctor Samuel Johnson can out-think and out-write your simple scribbler Tom Paine.

A Screenplay

> **BURT**
> It uh -- ss -- seems to me -- that Doctor Johnson and Mister Paine both have valid

> **VARICK**
> You can not sit on the fence your whole life Burt. You have to choose.

> **BURT**
> I ha -- have made a ch -- choice Richard. I—

> **JOSEPH**
> If you are to continue a friend to the farmer, Burt, you must be a friend to the King.

> **MRS. MCCREA**
> If you weren't my son Joseph I would drown you in the gravy. Have you the ability to shut that damnable barn door you call a mouth long enough for Burt to

> **JANE**
> Mother!

> **MRS. MCCREA**
>
> And you Richard. I've grown to love you these three years as if you were my own but when your brother is trying to state -- a pox on both your houses. You think to escape customs and taxes and (turns to Joseph) your king tries to act the parent

Betrayal

>   years after letting his children
>   run wild. Madness. If Samuel
>   Adams and Tom Paine and King
>   George and Lord North were all
>   thrown into Bedlam, they would
>   be happier. So would we all.

Hon Yost's high-pitched keening sound from outside interrupts.

Thomas and Jane open the door to investigate.

> THOMAS
> What is that awful noise?
> Someone's hurt. Where is my bag?

Hon Yost darts by the house spilling food from his plate.

Principal hurries just behind Hon Yost, slows to glance at Jane, and then calls to Yost.

> PRINCIPAL
> Pardonnez nous soft spirit.
> Pardonnez. Retournez, si vous
> plait.

Thomas finds his medical bag.

> JANE
> It's Mister Yost and Principal -
> - the serious Indian. No one's
> hurt. No work for you today,
> Tom. (She glances toward Varick
> and Joseph.) Not yet at least.

A Screenplay

> MRS. MCCREA
> Come back to table. We have a mountain of food to finish before we leave for afternoon service.

> MRS. MCCREA
> Jane, help me serve the pudding before Thomas expires -- of hunger. Shall we argue about who sits nearest Jane in the wagon. If we don't start fighting over that now, we'll never get to afternoon service on time.

All resume eating.

An awkward silence prevails.

> JANE
> I haven't told you Joseph about that great cow Lottie Smith. She went to visit her aunt in Boston for six months and came back with a baby niece.

> JOSEPH
> I have no interest in nieces. I've been away near a year Jane and -- whose war do you think you're fighting, Richard?

> JANE
> No one is suggesting that you are the father, Joseph. I'm merely warning you that she—

Betrayal

VARICK
I was fighting -- I am fighting -- I will fight here for the rights of Americans and Englishmen and all oppressed peoples of the world. I fight for the virtue of our cause..We will build a new order free of titles and -

JOSEPH
Virtue? Are you not fighting for an elite that will lump you with the unwashed rabble and scorn you? Do you rationally believe Benedict Arnold will invite you to his grand house in New Haven. Do you think that more respectable smuggler John Hancock will serve you tea by Boston Common. And your land-hungry mentor Phillip Schuyler -- will he entertain you in his governor's mansion or look the other way when he drives past in his fancy white coach?

VARICK
I think Sir that I shall be called upon to challenge your honor if you keep impugning the patriots I esteem!

Joseph is quiet a moment before responding.

JOSEPH
I see.

A Screenplay

> JANE
> This is... delicious, Mother.

> THOMAS
> Yes -- a blessing.

> JOSEPH
> I did not mean to cast aspersions on you, Richard, only your tarnished gods. But I take it poorly that in my own house, at my father's table, you, an esteemed guest, should try to stem my opinions with threats of violence.

Reverend McCrae looks up from his task of picking away at the turkey.

> REVEREND
> Guest? Your foster brother living here three years is a guest!

> JOSEPH
> This until now has always been a safe place for opinion, one of the last refuges for free speech in these colonies where one could disagree hotly but always trust in friendship to transcend all argument. Your conduct merely confirms my belief that those who shout for freedom shout only for their own.

Joseph stands up and throws his napkin on the table.

Betrayal

Reverend McCrae stands, moves to the wall behind him, and takes down a pistol.

                JOSEPH
   Goodbye Richard. I wish you safe
   journeys but never will we –

              REVEREND
   Sit down! I will shoot dead the
   first person who leaves this
   table in a heated state.

All are momentarily shocked into silence. Joseph sits.

Thomas starts to grin slowly.

              THOMAS
   If mother smiles and curtsies,
   might she go for the pudding
   sauce?

Thomas and Jane and Mrs. McCrae try to stifle grins.

             MRS. MCCREA
   Would you like the boys to sit a
   little closer, Dear, to improve
   your aim?

Burt hesitates between a smile and a frown. Joseph and Varick reluctantly smile.

Reverend McCrae lays down his pistol and sits.

              REVEREND
   I never could discipline any of
   you. That's why you've grown

A Screenplay

>   wild. I'm just an old bore
>   droning on about God's order
>   while the world is on fire.
>
>   MRS. MCCREA
>   Jedidiah, you are our light, our
>   beacon, our standard-bearer.

Reverend McCrae bows his head. Mrs. McCrae reaches for his hand.

>   JANE
>   You're not -- that old Father.
>   Don't touch that pistol, Mother.
>   I'll get the pudding sauce so
>   you and Old What's-His Name can
>   spark.

Jane skips out to the pantry.

Reverend McCrae can not help easing into a sad smile while shaking his head slowly.

All are smiling.

Burt stares worshipfully after Jane.

Simon Kirkland after Reverend's outburst -- leaves or--some minor role

EXT. SCHUYLER'S CAMP AT ALBANY - MORNING

Arnold and Schuyler are sipping brandy while grilling sausages, supplied by a servant, on sticks over a campfire.

In the background, a few Continental soldiers are sharpening axes, preparing torches, and making bullets.

Betrayal

Militia men are talking and clowning and shoving to get closer to the fires and grill their sausages.

A young corporal is frustrated in his attempts to drill a squad of militia who are more interested in the grilled sausages brought to them by their friends.

                SCHUYLER
John Stark has resigned, calling Congress a sorry collection of mental midgets. Another fighting general gone.

                ARNOLD
While Granny Gates takes your rightful position here in the northern department and Franklin plays the charming rustic for the powdered whores of the French court.

                SCHUYLER
Hmmmm. You know I am living in Beverly Robinson's house since he joined the British.

                ARNOLD
He is as fine a gentleman as you will find on either side.

                SCHUYLER
Yes. He recently sent me detailed instructions on turning his wine cellar for my better enjoyment. In less politically charged times, I would issue him a pass without a moment's

hesitation. But I am still watched closely by those who think our three thousand wretches at Ticonderoga should have scrapped with Burgoyne's nine thousand seasoned troops. If you should think it over –

                ARNOLD
I shall write the pass now while our sausages cook.

                SCHUYLER
It is not necessary to do it now. I meant only –

                ARNOLD
Is there ever a better moment than now. Pen! Ink! Paper!

Two servants leap into action digging into Schuyler's baggage.

                SCHUYLER
You are not a comfortable man with whom to hold a quiet reflection or think aloud, Benedict Arnold.

                ARNOLD
I shall endeavor, General Schuyler, to be quiet and comfortable in the grave, but I can not guarantee it. How do you spell Beverly?

Arnold exchanges his sausage on a stick with a servant who awkwardly hands him pen and paper and holds an ink bottle.

Betrayal

Arnold spins the servant around and uses his back for a writing board.

Schuyler enjoys the scene.

> SCHUYLER
> We have heard that John Burgoyne referred to our troops around Boston as ragamuffins. I am afraid I find that an apt description for these five hundred sorry soldiers I have assembled for you to lead to the relief of Fort Stanwix.

> ARNOLD
> Have they standard issue two arms and two legs? Can they aim and fire a musket? Perhaps Washington will loan us Daniel Morgan's rifle company.

> SCHUYLER
> We can not count on it. He has his own fish to fry.

> ARNOLD
> I will find a way. There. My compliments to Colonel Robinson.

Arnold hands the pass to Schuyler and studies the men on the field.

The squad continues to mostly ignore the commands of the corporal who is trying to maintain order and describe some drills.

A Screenplay

                    ARNOLD
          That corporal is a beginning. I
          can use persistent men.

                              CUT TO:

EXT. PRESBYTERIAN CHURCH AFTERNOON

Jane and Varick stand to one side observing
members of Reverend McCrae's congregation
who are finishing up picnic dinners or just
arriving for afternoon service.

Burt helps a woman and child climb down
from their wagon.

Thomas in full dress blue Continental Army
uniform with ornamental sword by his side
greets his loud rebel friends who arrive on
horseback.

Mrs. McCrae is chatting with several women.

Joseph, wearing a white garter on his
uniform sleeve, stands apart and nods
occasionally to Tory acquaintances who form
a floating group and whisper to each other.

                    VARICK
          ...and just as I'm telling the
          sergeants to keep their heads
          and travel light Granny Gates
          goes flying out of Fort
          Ticonderoga as if The Headless
          Horseman were after him --
          ignoring his aides who are
          trying to pile half the fort on
          pack horses.

Jane and Varick laugh.

> JANE
> I love your stories, Richard, but I'm worried about Burton longing to go to war. He has no business there. I could never forgive myself if he could never forgive you.

> VARICK
> Me? Why do you anoint me with such guilt? I want him home rebuilding our farm where he belongs.

> JANE
> You're the half-brother he worships and adores, riding in and out of his life, smelling of gunpowder and danger. You act on your beliefs -- he thinks himself a coward if he does not... damn your stories.

> VARICK
> I'll talk to him in due time. I think I may be home to stay, Jane. I have done my part. Come to the belfry.

A large young lady LOTTIE SMITH alights from her carriage.

She hands the baby she is carrying to a servant and goes directly to Joseph.

A Screenplay

JANE
I tried to warn Joseph about
Lottie Smith but he's too full
of himself. Puts me in mind of a
Continental Army lieutenant I
know. Look at her mooing away.
I'd rather Joseph marry our milk
cow.

VARICK
Perhaps a former Continental
Army lieutenant. Gates is bad
enough galloping off at the
first sign of battle, but
Phillip Schuyler -- I served
with Schuyler for more than a
year, part of his family really
-- and not one mention of
political plans. Not one.

JANE
A wise man holds his own
counsel.

VARICK
I shall. From now on. (Jane
smiles briefly.) Benedict Arnold
is the only fierce fighting
general we have but they say he
dissipates his energies with
young Tory girls and money
schemes... I have done my part.

JANE
His great appetites are not
confined to young girls. When he
stopped here on his way to
Valcour last year -- he got
through undressing me with his

eyes, took Mother for a long walk and perhaps undressed –

                    VARICK
Jane!
                    JANE
Richard. They were gone two hours and Mother's hair was mussed and her dress –

                    VARICK
Jane, that's your mother you're slandering.

                    JANE
Slandering? How quaint. I thought I was admiring. You poor innocent. Want to dance with the devil? Find a minister's daughter.

Jane smiles briefly.

Varick wears a serious, pained look.

                    VARICK
Come to the belfry.

                    JANE
I will if you promise to talk. There are many things need saying.

                    VARICK
Of course.

A Screenplay

> JANE
> Don't 'of course' me. And don't get your hopes or anything else up.

> VARICK
> Jane, I have suffered for you. I have never even –

> JANE
> Please Varick. This incessant self-pitying chatter drives me to distraction.

> VARICK
> Chatter!

> JANE
> Father has been preaching goodness and mercy to me for nigh twenty-three years. You rant on about independence these three years to every male in the county. To me you recite calendar days with your prick in your pants. Saint Varick the Abstinent. My hero. Saving his seed for—

> VARICK
> Jane, what have I done to deserve such scorn? I love you.

> JANE
> I think you try to, but does your notion of love allow any room for--
> The church bell rings.

Betrayal

Lottie Smith takes Joseph's arm.

              VARICK
  Come Jane. At best we only have
  a little time to -

              JANE
  Talk. You promised to talk.

                        MOVE TO:

INT. PRESBYTERIAN CHURCH ALTAR AFTERNOON

The choir is singing "Chester.".

Reverend Jedidiah McCrae fidgets with his gown and is turning down pages of his Bible and scribbling notes on strips of white paper.

Reverend McCrae stands and moves to the pulpit before realizing that the choir has not finished singing.

He sits and fidgets and then signals them to finish quickly.

He rises and places on the lectern his Bible which has paper markers sticking out every which way.

              REVEREND
  I fought the Stamp Act and I
  would again... it is right for
  you to ask: could Reverend
  McCrea be hoping for a healing
  of the schism with the Church of
  England? NO! Does he believe us
  a more virtuous people than the

A Screenplay

    guilt-laden societies of Europe?
    YES! The prejudices we suffered
    -

Mrs. McCrae nervously watches him and members of the congregation who strain to understand his meaning.

Varick and Jane reach the last step of the winding stairs to the belfry. Varick embraces Jane who is trying to hear her father's words which rise and fall.

              REVEREND
    (O.S.) -- we do not choose a
    Parliament-driven worship... Had
    we needed a great awakening Our
    Lord would have...

Richard unbuttons and kisses and caresses Jane who resists feebly.

              JANE
    Father started early. No
    Richard. We have to talk. Much
    has -- ahhh -- don't -touch me
    like that. We should go down.
    NOOO...

              REVEREND
    (O.S.) ... why can't we meet the
    King's peace commissioners? New
    Lights, Old Lights, New Sides.
    Many of us -- most have never
    been asleep -- need no
    awakening... the latest
    whimsical trappings of a suspect
    spirituality... seen village
    sots elevated to statesmen --

> let the young search... God has reasons that we do not understand. It is his order that we must adhere to. If a father goes astray should we then abandon him or gently lead him back to the bosom of his family? Should we find virtue in God or in man's puny attempts at forms of order called government? I have tried to minister to all even as I see some trodding the path of viciousness...

JANE
> I have missed you too, Richard, but we really mustn't don't take advantage of my sinfulness yess –

REVEREND
> (O.S.) ... we do not choose a Parliament-driven worship... Had we needed a great awakening Our Lord would have... did I say...

DISSOLVE TO:

INT. PRESBYTERIAN CHURCH PULPIT – LATE AFTERNOON Reverend McCrae is looking around for his Bible.

Thinking that he has finished his sermon, the choir stands and opens their hymn books.

He finds his Bible right next to him on the pulpit.

A Screenplay

                REVEREND
  Ahh!

He holds up his Bible and waves it and begins to speak before noticing the choir.

                REVEREND
    I stand with Isaiah -- please be seated.

The choir sits down.

He holds up his Bible and waves it and shouts.

                REVEREND
    I love my daughter and my foster son -even as they trod a path I find -- I stand with Isaiah: 'I have nourished children and brought them up and even they have revolted from me!'

INT. PRESBYTERIAN CHURCH BELFRY - LATE AFTERNOON

In the belfry Varick is lying beside Jane who is crying silently as she starts to button her dress. He rises on his elbow to hear better.

                VARICK
    He's talking about me, Jenny -- I think.
                JANE
    No. Burton and I. I wanted to tell you. We have become New Christians of the Two Lights. And we have been... walking out.

Betrayal

VARICK
Burt! My own half-brother! And you -- I'm fighting a war for freedom   and behind my back you -- my intended my Burt -how -

JANE
Shhh, Richard. This will be our last visit to the belfry for -- I was weak -oh, please -- don't look at me like that. I felt I owed -- we must go down.

VARICK
Why did you bring me here?

REVEREND
(O.S.)...God has his reasons for the order he has established. I have seen prudent men in our valley tarred and feathered by the refuse of taverns. It can not be God's Will! I cannot abide the persecution of good men and women! Destruction of property because they believe in gradual versus violent reform. We welcome all here but -- I speak now a man of (as?) Christian sensibilities! A citizen of these colonies!

VARICK
You let me -- you led me to -

A Screenplay

INT. PRESBYTERIAN CHURCH (PULPIT) - LATE AFTERNOON Reverend McCrae pauses and has trouble continuing.

> REVEREND
> ...render unto God -- worship the God who is God... and... render unto Caesar that which -- is Ceasar's--
> Reverend McCrae tries to pull off his minister's frock. It gets caught.

He tears it as he reveals the green uniform of a Tory colonel of militia underneath.

> REVEREND
> I am remain a loyal subject of King George the Third!

The church erupts in confusion.

Several Tories scattered throughout the congregation rise to voice approval.

A small knot of rebels sitting on the left side of the church rise in unison to hiss and boo.

Most members talk or whisper to their family and friends as the Reverend tries to continue.

Jane, followed reluctantly by Varick, remembers to finish buttoning her dress as she rushes down the center aisle to the altar.

Betrayal

>   REVEREND
>   Yea though I walk through the
>   valley of the shadow of death I
>   shall fear no evil. Thy rod and
>   thy staff they comfort me... are
>   we to act as parricides...

Mrs. McCrae and Burt go up to the pulpit to bring the Reverend down.

Jane and Joseph turn to face the rebel contingent bearing down on the altar.

Thomas and Varick step in front of Jane and Joseph as the rebels' spokesman YOUNG HERKIMER erupts.

>   YOUNG HERKIMER
>   You would protect that Tory
>   viper -- that false prophet --
>   that foolish old man. Does he
>   think the Mohawks will burn only
>   half his house!

>   VARICK
>   I wish not to kill you Young
>   Herkimer.

Thomas draws his sword and holds it awkwardly

>   THOMAS
>   No. I shall cut out his tongue
>   and sew it back only when he
>   remembers who baptized him.

A Screenplay

All pause as Mrs. McCrae and Burt lead the Reverend down the steps to stand at the head of the aisle. He is befuddled.

          REVEREND
...Yea though I walk through the valley of the shadow of death I shall fear no -lie down beside the still waters -- evil -- I know these youths -- that is Nicolas Herkimer's son and that is -- ahh -Thomas's friend -- do we not know them Mother? Burton? Jenny?

          BURT
Th -- they are our friends Father.

Young Herkimer hesitates. He steps aside.

Others follow his example.

Varick lingers and stares hatefully as Reverend McCrae is led from the church.

          JOSEPH
Come away, Richard. You are not a duellist. If you keep staring at those men, one will surely challenge you.

          VARICK
I am not staring. I am remembering.

(End of second Hour)

EXT. VARICK FARM AND ADJOINING MCCRAE FARM - DAY SERIES OF SHOTS

A) Richard Varick is riding along the border of the McCrae and Varick farms striking authoritative poses as Thomas and Joseph smile at his efforts from a distance

Varick starts to interrupt a solitary farmhand's work to ask a question, but sees that it is Burt, and turns away as Burt watches him go

Varick, dozing with an open Bible, wakes to find a dandelion necklace on his chest.

Varick holds soil in his hand, looks around to see that no one is watching, and throws the soil away.

EXT. MCCRAE FARM - NOON

Jane on horseback leaves messages and the noon meal in the crook of the maple tree and rides slowly toward Varick.

He wheels about and rides off as Jane calls.

              JANE
Richard, you're acting the ass!

            VARICK
How could you let me

              JANE
I was weak. I was sinful. I was needful. Burt and I have yet to —

A Screenplay

> **VARICK**
> Oh. So that's it. I was just a convenience. My half-brother and my intended are purely platonic lovers. I am needed only to provide hard flesh as required.

> **JANE**
> That's hateful, Richard. Why do I
> struggle with a choice between a sweet plain man and a nasty revolutionary with inflated opinions of himself.

> **VARICK**
> It looks to me as if the struggle is only in your fancy.

> **JANE**
> It is now. Thank you for helping me to decide against you.

Jane spurs her horse and calls back.

> **JANE**
> I detest you.

> **VARICK**
> Thank you. I could not ask for more -detestation by a falsely religious strumpet.

DISSOLVE TO: EXT. MCCRAE FARMYARD - MORNING

Burt is mounted on his horse which Hon Yost leads toward the family gathered in front of the house.

Betrayal

Principal ranges ahead after looking at Jane.

Second Runner tries to keep up with Principal and talks softly to his back.

> VARICK
> Where is Burt going with the half-wit? Jane? Thomas?

> HON YOST
> Raspberry picking.

> BURT
> Guh -- goodbye, Richard. I'm guh -- going for Burgoyne.

> VARICK
> What! You are joining the enemy. What would Mother think?

> JANE
> She would think that her younger son has purchased a commission in the proud British army of George the Third. She would think that her son Richard and my brother Joseph have driven him to it with their mad certain pontifications. Who appointed you the sons of God?

> JOSEPH
> I deeply respect Burt's decision to—

> VARICK
> Every fibre of my being rejects Burt's

A Screenplay

                    JANE
Shut your mouth! You pompous
fools! Burton has no business on
battlefields. He is a gentle
farmer willing to listen to all
views, but you won't let him.
You won't—

                    BURT
Jane, be easy. I must go for
King George, Richard. I am sorry
to disappoint you. Joseph,
Thomas, I will ss -- sorely miss
you. God bless and preserve all
here.

                    JANE
Oh God!

                SECOND RUNNER
I only speak the truth, my
brother.

                    BURT
Though I leave against your
hopes, may -may I still call you
Father and Mother, Reverend
McCrea? Moth -- Mrs. McCrea?

With tears in his eyes Reverend McCrea nods
assent.

                 MRS. MCCREA
Good God! They're taking my
sweet boy away. Call me anything
you like but come home in one
piece. I will slice Burgoyne in
a stew if anything happens.

Betrayal

                    BURT
          I --I luh -- I -- I love you all
          dearly and could not imagine my
          world without you.

Jane runs to Burt and nearly pulls him off
his horse to kiss him on the lips.

Varick glares at Burt who blushes and
stares at the ground. Joseph looks
quizzically after Jane who runs off.

                    THOMAS
          Safe home.

                    HON YOST
          Red berries.

INT. MCCRAE HOUSE - MORNING

Richard Varick, Jane McCrae, and Mrs.
McCrae sit silently at the breakfast table.

Reverend McCrae sits in a rocking chair by
the fire ignoring the open Bible in his lap.

Hoofbeats are heard.

Varick and Jane rise simultaneously.

Jane sits down as Varick goes to the door
to meet the messenger.

                    DISPATCH RIDER
          I am, per order of General
          Arnold, to give this only to
          Richard Varick.

A Screenplay

                    VARICK
    I am he.

Mrs. McCrae fixes a cup of tea and slices
bread for the dispatch rider as Varick
reads the message.

                    [INSERT]
        We HEAR Arnold's voice as Varick
        READS:
        ARNOLD (V.O.)
        "Lieutenant Varick, I need a man
        of enterprise."
        "Your efforts last year to get
        me supplies for the Valcour
        Island encounter when none else
        would have indelibly stamped you
        in my mind as a man of
        exertions. Come to me on the
        march. I leave Albany for
        Stillwater en route to Fort
        Stanwix. Burgoyne is rewarding
        the savages for any scalp they
        lift. Your country needs you. I
        most certainly do."
        "General Benedict Arnold"

Mrs. McCrea looks at Varick who clenches
his fist around the message.

She tries to engage Jane's attention but
she looks away.

                                   CUT TO:

EXT. BURGOYNE'S CAMP - MORNING

Soldiers are lounging about in small groups
swapping stories. Carpenters are building a

huge stage in the near background. To the
rear officers' children are playing.

In the far background casual camp life with
soldiers and women gambling, haggling,
cooking, jostling, arguing goes on.

Burt dismounts, hands his orders to
Sergeant Burbank.

              BURT
    I mu -- must see General
    Burgoyne. Mm -my orders are to
    report to him.

          SERGEANT BURBANK
    Of course you do, Son. (Reads
    orders.) Uh, Captain. Now follow
    me and I'll find a proper major
    to assist you. (Walks ahead
    toward main camp.) You are the
    first of many Mohawk Valley
    officers we expect to join us.
    Did you have an easy journey?

After a few steps and no response, Sergeant
Burbank turns to see Burt headed directly
for the stage.

          SERGEANT BURBANK
    You can't bother General
    Burgoyne! Colonel Phillips! Stop
    that young fool! Please. Sir.
    (Sees Principal and Second
    Runner slipping into the woods.)
    Stop him, you louts!

Burgoyne is pacing, straining the limits of
a small temporary stage, and instructing

A Screenplay

his mistress who is seated on a chair with extra cushions. Both hold script pages.

              BURGOYNE
    You must pout and stomp and heave your bosom, My Dear. The great actresses are also the great exhibitionists. And you have the charms to exhibit.

Burgoyne turns to see Phillips reading Burt's orders as Sergeant Burbank catches up and reaches from behind to restrain Burt.

              BURGOYNE
    What is this rumpus, Phillips?

              PHILLIPS
    A young Loyalist, Your Excellency, Burton Timmons of the Mohawk valley with a regular captain's commission, who thinks reporting to your army requires reporting to you. I'll have him removed.

              BURGOYNE
    No, no. Perhaps we require a diversion. This playacting is a dry business. Wine! Come up, Young Sir! How do you do. May I be of service. Let me introduce you to my friend.

Burt climbs the stairs and bows awkwardly to Burgoyne's mistress.

Betrayal

Arthur brings a decanter of wine and three glasses on a tray. He stands nearby and stares at Burt throughout.

> BURT
> How do y -- you dhhh -- my nn -- ame iss

> BURGOYNE
> No need to be worrisome about names. We are all friends here joined in a great expedition to ensure the felicity of all Englishmen under His Gracious Majesty George the Third. How come you here?

> BURT
> Mr. Hon Yost and his Indian fr - - frri-- ends brow -- brought me.

> BURGOYNE
> (Smiling.) Of course they did. You are most welcome. We expect to add two thousand loyal subjects like you as we march toward Albany. No need for shyness here. Kiss your cousin and—

> BURT
> I would beg a favor, Your Highness.

Burgoyne talks in soft asides to his mistress and a loud voice to Burt.

A Screenplay

BURGOYNE
(Aside) But newly arrived and a favor already. What, pray tell, shall we do to make you more welcome. (Aside) And I thought the pumpkin shy.

BURT
I humbly ask permission to send for my fiancee, Jane McCrea, daughter of Reverend and Mrs. Jedidiah McCrae.

BURGOYNE
Yes! Splendid! Colonel Baum's good wife has asked for help in managing the officers' children. Will you marry soon?

BURT
We would be most honored if Your Grace would marry us in Albany.

BURGOYNE
(Aside.) His campaign is better designed than my army's. I think I shall be happy to do that. If the rabble keep running, we will be there in—

BURT
Th -- theyyy wo -- wove k -- keeepp running. S -- ss --s ir.

BURGOYNE
(Aside.) Now my premier military advisor. (Mistress giggles loudly.) Thank you for the illumination. Now, have you the

time and the wish to, I am sure
that Major—

              BURT
Cou -- could you please send
Mister Hon Yost and his Indian
friends to escort Jane here. She
knows him and would be easy in
their company.

            BURGOYNE
Shall we -

Burgoyne pauses between annoyance and
amusement. He chooses the latter and bows
with a flourish.

            BURGOYNE
-- review? Your fiancee is
welcome to join our march. I
shall begin preparations to join
you in matrimony in Albany. I
should expect the rebels'
resistance to stiffen; rather,
to make its first appearance,
and Mister Yost and Indian
friends has been designated for
escort duty. Have you aught else
for me to do this morning?

Arthur smiles broadly, catches himself, and
resumes a neutral demeanor.

            BURT
(staring at his shoes) N - nuh
no, Ss -- Sir. G -- Geh --
General. Th-thank you. (looks up
at Burgoyne.) Jane and I thank
you from the bottom of our

hearts, Your Excellency. (looks down) I -- I'd b -- best go.

Burgoyne stares after Burt who shuffles off obediently behind Sergeant Burbank.

                    BURGOYNE
Is this colonial air charged with more than Franklin's electricity? Who breeds these shy, bold, impertinent rustics-- and he, loyal to our standard, thinks highly of his rabble countrymen who oppose us. Well, he is certain wrong. We will fix bayonets, strike up a minuet and dance softly down to Albany. Phillips, keep all such colonial princes from me. Such impudence. I was two years a major before I dared ask my commanding officer for anything. Now, in the second act, My Princess -- ah, is it nap time. I shan't resist you.

                    PHILLIPS
But -- Your Excellency, I have the first draft of your instructions to the Mohawks.

                    BURGOYNE
How -- nice. Revise it, Phillips. Make it -- the second draft. Then I shall peruse it.

                    PHILLIPS
Sir? (Salutes.) Sir!

Burgoyne waves a hurried half-salute half-flourish. He follows his mistress into their day tent. Arthur continues to stare after Burt.

EXT. ARNOLD'S CAMP - EVENING

Varick rides into Arnold's camp which has a decided air of order and industry.

Soldiers are drilling clumsily or learning to clean muskets.

Officers and NCOs are reading manuals or studying maps and newspapers by candle light.

A cooper is finishing a barrel.

Women are cooking, airing blankets, and washing laundry.

Varick dismounts and enters the largest tent which has rolled and tied flaps.

Franks is leaning over a table full of papers. He looks up. Varick salutes.

                    FRANKS
You are?

                    VARICK
Lieutenant Richard Varick from the Mohawk Valley.

                    FRANKS
How grand. I am Major Franks of the Philadelphia Franks.

A Screenplay

Varick offers to shake hands.

Franks quickly imprisons the ends of Varick's fingers and releases them immediately.

>   VARICK
> Is General Arnold present?

>   FRANKS
> Our Little General has dubbed
> you 'a man of exertions.' He's -
> - ahh -- awaiting you anxiously
> in the small tent just behind
> this.

>   VARICK
> Thank you.

>   FRANKS
> Il ny a pas de quoi.

Varick walks briskly beside headquarters tent.

He hears noises and a shrill laugh as he stops outside a small gaily-colored tent with closed flaps.

>   VARICK
> General Arnold! It is I, Richard
> Varick, from the Mohawk Valley.

He listens to scuffling noises in the tent and short shrill bursts of laughter.

>   ARNOLD
> Let go of that. Stop it.

Betrayal

Arnold rushes out of the tent feigning annoyance.

He pulls the flaps closed behind him and straightens his hose.

As he returns Varick's salute, a young girl of fifteen, half dressed, pulls open the flaps and salutes Arnold's back.

>ARNOLD
> Lieutenant Varick, welcome to my headquarters.

>ALINDA
> My Little General! Welcome back to my headquarters. Any time soon. And bring Mister Mohawk Valley with you. Or send him ahead.

Leaning back from Arnold's breath and staring at Alinda's exposed breasts, Varick is speechless.

>ALINDA
> Can we count? Still two? No need to take off your boots for this sum?
> Arnold is looking over his shoulder at his stockings.

>ARNOLD
> Are they straight? (sees Varick staring) Get away, Girl, and cover up. Don't be acting the part of a trollop.

A Screenplay

                    ALINDA
   Acting?

Alinda blows Varick a kiss and retires into her tent laughing shrilly.

Varick picks up his pace to catch up and keep up with Arnold.

                            CUT TO:

EXT. MOHAWK VALLEY MILITIA CAMP BY ORISKANY CREEK - NIGHT

GENERAL NICOLAS HERKIMER is filling his pipe frenetically, dropping his tobacco pouch, failing to strike a light, giving up in disgust.

His son Young Herkimer watches him.

They both are listening to the grumblings of their farmer friends who are impatient with delay.

                FARMERS' VOICES
   I have cows to milk... corn to
   harvest... If his brother Hans
   fought with us... We would have
   been there now... And back...
   wheat to dry... He is not a
   turncoat... Butwhy...

                   HERKIMER
   Who made these farmers so noisy?
   Joseph Brandt has quieter
   councils with all six nations of
   the Iroquois speaking.

Betrayal

YOUNG HERKIMER
They will go home, Father -- I am sorry -- General Herkimer. They think you hesitate because Uncle Hans fights for St. Leger at Stanwix.

HERKIMER
We must wait yet a while. I have my good reasons.

YOUNG HERKIMER
They want to fire their muskets once and go home.

HERKIMER
Your uncle fights for the British. I fight for our country. I make no decisions based on brotherhood.

YOUNG HERKIMER
We must march now or they will take harvest leave. They are more worried about feeding their families than afraid. They have work to do.

HERKIMER
I am a farmer. I know this. We must work with the men in the fort and Benedict Arnold who will be marching our way... soon. Or we will have farms full of widows. I have sent an Oneida. We must wait... all right, I will have a council of officers. I will convince them that we will -- we must -- wait.

A Screenplay

Herkimr claps his hands to get attention.

CUT TO:

EXT. ARNOLD'S CAMP - AFTERNOON

Varick is having trouble keeping up with Arnold who walks briskly despite a noticeable limp.

Franks follows closely enough to hear the conversation.

                ARNOLD
    Despite young men's wishes and
    the tavern ballads, persuasion
    and prudence are often keys to
    leadership. I have sent to
    Washington to loan me Daniel
    Morgan and his sharpshooters in
    accordance with my officers'
    vote in council.

                VARICK
    What are the odds, Sir?

Arnold checks his stockings.

                ARNOLD
    Pure silk, Lieutenant Varick.
    The British Colonel Barry St.
    Leger has a force of 2,000 but
    my agents tell me more than half
    are Mohawks who see no
    compelling reason to die for
    King George.

Betrayal

Major Franks joins them. He adopts a French accent.

> FRANKS
> You will, si vous plait, Mon General, tell the young officer of our fierce fighting might?

> ARNOLD
> Four hundred firm men in the fort and several hundred drabs. Herkimer comes with 800 farmers. If we can strike at the exact same moment with our five hundred, we are almost equal in numbers -- should our militia acquit themselves well -

> FRANKS
> Oui, Mon General. We would have more than fifteen hundred militia who, if we are trés fortunate, will fire one shot before runnning from Mohawk hatchets and British bayonets. They will be food for the wolves in the woods around Fort Stanwix. It is certainment, Mon Grand Jehn -- air -- ahl.

Franks finishes with a bow and a flourish.

> ARNOLD
> Should you choose to repeat those little French flourishes, you will be butchered in these woods. (to Varick) major Franks is certain that the French will join us against the British if

A Screenplay

> we can win just one decisive
> battle. He twits me on my
> distrust of the French and their
> Popish ways. If we must use
> them, we must, but I well
> remember -- (ahh?)that was then
> and this is now...

Arnold spots Sullivan who is polishing his huge hunting knife and speaking and gesturing to a somber, nodding Piggott who is writing copious notes.

> ARNOLD
>> Sergeant Sullivan!
>
> SULLIVAN
>> Sir!

Sullivan sheathes his knife and runs toward Arnold and Varick whom he recognizes with a smile.

> ARNOLD
>> I have a critical assignment for
>> you and Lieutenant Varick. You
>> two are
>> acquainted?
>
> VARICK
>> Yes, we—
>
> SULLIVAN
>> Did you know, Sir, you bear a
>> remarkable resemblance to a
>> young officer who retired into
>> the Mohawk Valley ages ago --
>> perhaps a full ten days You must
>> be a cousin? Old Varick is it?

Betrayal

VARICK
No, it is not. I will thank you to address –

ARNOLD
Enough! Go to General Herkimer. He was en route to Fort Stanwix via Oriskany Creek. Tell Herkimer he must wait. I have couriers to Washington. Herkimer must not attack alone. He is a staunch man but sensitive that his brother fights for the British.

SULLIVAN
Sir!

VARICK
I understand perfect –

ARNOLD
On your return stop at William Pitt Tavern and recruit me some seasoned musket men. I shall not wait forever even for Washington. If he could spare troops from countering Sir William Howe's every move he should have done so by now.

VARICK
Shall we set out in the morning?

ARNOLD
Why would you waste half a day?

A Screenplay

                    VARICK
          Uh -- Sir! We will leave this
          very afternoon.

Arnold frowns at Varick and turns away.

                    ARNOLD
          Franks! Are my hose ready? Has
          my shipment arrived? Why are the
          men not drilling? Where are my
          letters?

                    SULLIVAN
          Our Little General is not a
          patient gardener, Sir. Once he
          plants the seed for action he
          expects an immediate
          harvest.(calls) We ride with
          this breeze Your Worship! (to
          Varick) He means now.

                    VARICK
          Am I afforded the courtesy of
          stowing my gear in my tent.

                    SULLIVAN
          No. This is a flexible camp.
          When we come back -- if we come
          back -- Franks will find a cot
          for you. I have piled your
          baggage in headquarters tent for
          the moment.

As Varick mounts he notices Piggott
fashioning large lariats with loose knots
as he consults his notes.

Betrayal

> VARICK
> He's not coming, is he?

> SULLIVAN
> Unless you insist. No. Piggott
> now protects the perimeter of
> camp.

> VARICK
> Thank God for little favors.

> SULLIVAN
> Do I detect a newly religious
> note? Not hoping to replace your
> foster father now that he has
> declared himself a flaming Tory?

> VARICK
> How did you know of that?

> SULLIVAN
> Ahh, the trees and I have ears
> everywhere. And we have all of
> Piggott's relatives. Shall we?
> If you care to say a fond
> au'voir to the General...

Varick turns his horse and starts for headquarters tent.

He sees Arnold gesturing and spewing out orders before realizing that Sullivan is joking.

Varick rides to catch up with and go ahead of Sullivan.

A Screenplay

EXT. BRITISH SIEGE CAMP OUTSIDE FORT STANWIX - EVENING
Mohawks in suits and derby hats from London tailors are talking, smoking, arguing.

Others in loincloths are wrestling or playing lacrosse.

British Regulars dig slant siege ditches zigzagging toward Fort Stanwix.

General St. Leger is pacing, looking as if he might interrupt the soldiers' work, and talking to Chief Joseph Brandt who turns slowly and steadily to keep St. Leger in sight.

              ST.LEGER
Why are they wearing those suits and hats? They look ludicrous, godawful. Why can't they help my men dig closer? Did they expect high tea here at Fort Stanwix?

             CHIEF JOSEPH
We were told of smooth journeys and treasures for our longhouses. Did The Great Burgoyne forget to tell Colonel St. Leger that his Redcoats were to do the hard fighting?

              ST.LEGER
Appointed General St. Leger for this mission. No warrior expects a pass during dangerous times. Not with Arnold loose near the Valley.

Betrayal

CHIEF JOSEPH
Where are the British Redcoats?
I count less than three hundred.
(and?) Six hundred angry Tories
who will not wash in the creek
near my men. That leaves my
Mohawks, 1200 captains and
warriors, pride of The Six
Nations, to die for Third
George. The suits and hats he
gave us in London do not make
sufficient reward for the death
of our nations. We are brought
here to scare a few sorry
militia in Fort Stanwix. Not to
dig in the earth.

ST.LEGER
That was our intelligence. We
did not count on the rebels
refusing to even discuss terms
of surrender.

CHIEF JOSEPH
Soon my Mohawks will face their
brothers the Oneidas who come
this way with Nicholas
Herkimer's rebel farmers. Must
we learn from you British to
kill our brothers more fiercely
than strangers or slaves.

ST.LEGER
Fortunes of war. And if your
foolish Oneidas and Tuscaroras
choose to believe diseased
preachers like Simon Kirkland
that is your lookout.

A Screenplay

In the background Sergeant Burbank rides in, dismounts, and confers with The Young Private who points to an Indian at the edge of (the fire)?light.

        CHIEF JOSEPH
Must we deserve to vanish from this earth for our misplaced trust. Is not Simon Kirkland your preacher? Are not they all your preachers? Your brothers?

        ST.LEGER
I can not be responsible for traitorous clergymen. That would be akin to your being responsible for the actions of every warrior in The Six Nations.

        CHIEF JOSEPH
I am -- I was... How should it be else?

Sergeant Burbank hurries in and salutes St. Leger.

        SERGEANT BURBANK
Sir, Sergeant Burbank reporting. General Burgoyne sends his best wishes but can spare no long cannon. Also, a warrior to see Chief Brandt. His markings are smudged -- I think Oneida and something else. He—

        ST.LEGER
Bring him into the light.

Betrayal

> SERGEANT BURBANK
> He seems ready to bolt. Some news about Herkimer with rebel militia near Oriskany Creek -- it might be best if Chief Joseph—

> CHIEF JOSEPH
> Thank you Sergeant. I will go to him.

Burbank begins to salute Brandt, catches himself, turns slightly to face and salute St. Leger.

St. Leger steps forward.

> ST.LEGER
> You are dismissed Sergeant. You may go to the Oneida, Chief Brandt.

> CHIEF JOSEPH
> Thank you, General St. Leger, ever so much.

EXT. MOHAWK VALLEY WOODS DAY

Varick strives to keep up with and copy Sullivan who is riding ahead quietly, alertly. Varick calls.

> VARICK
> I noticed in Philadelphia that you had varied and broad acquaintance -- Joseph Reed, Samuel Adams -

A Screenplay

              SULLIVAN
I served nine years in the
British army and now two in this
Continental -assemblage
(mishmash/potpourri?). One makes
acquaintances. Is there a point
to be made?

              VARICK
No -- no point -- I merely --
Sullivan stops, turns, comes
back to Varick, rides around
him.

              SULLIVAN
I had hoped to speak plain with
you soon enough, Richard Varick.
This time will serve.

Sullivan's serious manner bothers Varick.

              VARICK
Plain about which? If you are
part of the Conway cabal—

              SULLIVAN
would that I were. I hear --
does this Congress pay you too
much too often, Lieutenant
Varick? I have not been paid
these nine months. The babes do
not live on air. When I am paid,
no one here or in County Cork
will exchange that cursed paper
for anything of value. I hurt no
one to speak of. If tidbits of
gossip from Arnold's camp are
worth good hard specie to

certain politicians, I will
tidbit them to death.

                VARICK
You spy on Arnold and he trusts
you unresevedly! Have you no
honor, no shame!

                SULLIVAN
Arnold has a broad back and a
sharp intelligence. I am sure
that he employs spies to spy on
me. Perhaps you are one?

                VARICK
I am not! I would never stoop so
low. Nor would General Arnold.
Sullivan dismounts and walks his
horse beside Varick's.

                SULLIVAN
Where did we raise you, Old
Varick. Every officer I've
served, British and Continental,
uses information for his own
betterment. I should, were I
you, stop worrying about stature
and start earning true money for
my darling's wedding dress by
listening-

                VARICK
I prefer not to discuss my
arrangements with Miss McCrae.

                SULLIVAN
Ahhh, threw you over, did she?
Must be a market for that
tidbit. Should you decide to

toil in the vineyards of information, I do know gentlemen eager to pay substantial sums for intimate details of General Arnold's financial arrangements, letters of agreement, receipts, etcetera. Information I am rarely privy to.

                VARICK
Joseph Reed no doubt is one.

                SULLIVAN
Should I tell you all I know, Lieutenant Varick, and forego any chance of earning sustaining money for the wife and babes? I think not. A few regular entries in this journal –

Sullivan takes a journal from his saddlebag, thrusts it at Varick, mounts quickly and rides ahead.

                VARICK
How can you live within yourself being disloyal to Arnold and –

                SULLIVAN
I am loyal. To my Toms -- Paine and Jefferson -- at least to some of their ideas. For the rest of it, a man must do as he must (spurs his horse and calls back) -- a universal truth known round the world excepting a certain corner of the Mohawk Valley.

Betrayal

              VARICK
In my corner of the Mohawk
Valley we prize fidelity and
trustworthiness. A man is what
he seems -- I don't want this --
this -

Sullivan reins his horse and listens.

              SULLIVAN
Hold! Down.

Sullivan slides off his horse.

Varick thrusts the jounal into his saddlebag, jumps, falls, rolls.

Sullivan points to the top of a small hill.

They crawl up.

Distant sounds of battle can be heard faintly.

Sullivan looks briefly through a spyglass and hands it to Varick.

Through the spyglass Varick sees a militia man fire his musket and start to reload.

              SULLIVAN
(O.S.) Herkimer's in rough
circumstances. We must get to
him. It's coming on to rain
hard.

Through the spyglass Varick sees a Mohawk split the militia man's head with a tomahawk and scalp him.

A Screenplay

                    VARICK
          Oh my God!

Sullivan tugs on Varick's arm.

As they mount, lightning and thunder erupt and pouring rain drenches them instantly.

EXT. ORISKANY CREEK - DAY

General Nicolas Herkimer is trying to rally and re-order his militia on higher ground as the rain storm increases in intensity.

                    HERKIMER
          Twos! Form and fight by twos!
          One fire, one load. Twos!

Herkimer is hit in the leg, falls. He is dragged up a knoll as the thunderstorm rages.

All combatants look for shelter and try to keep their powder dry.

Under cover of the storm Sullivan and Varick reach Herkimer who is propped up against a fallen tree smoking his pipe.

                    VARICK
          General Herkimer I am Lieutenant
          Richard Varick come direct from
          General Arnold to—

                    HERKIMER
          Young Richard. No. Lieutenant
          Varick now. You were a boy when

your father served with me. He was my most reliable scout. You wanted to run away with us. we—

VARICK
General Arnold—

HERKIMER
Urges me to wait. I did not wait. Arnold will understand. I stood to lose many men who thought I hesitated because my brother fights for the British at Fort Stanwix. I sent an Oneida to give the men in the fort a signal when we could attack together. He has not come back. we were ambushed.

SULLIVAN
Excuse me Sir! The rain is letting up.

HERKIMER
Thank you Sergeant. Get the men fighting in twos. When the rain stops it is our only chance. They are good and stubborn German farmers. Curse them. Beat them. Save their lives.

SULLIVAN
Sir!

Sullivan stands and turns to the militia men who have waited in small groups to see how Herkimer is doing.

A Screenplay

SULLIVAN
All right My Honeys, pair off.
Two to a tree, a rock, a log.
Double up. One fires while the
other loads. Move! Or I'll bash
your head in and scalp you
myself!

MILITIA MAN
Who are you to order us abou--
Sullivan clubs the man with the
butt of his musket and steps
over him. Most of the militia
begin to pair off. One
hesitates. Sullivan pulls his
huge hunting knife from its
sheath.

SULLIVAN
Twos My Honey Boy or I'll carve
my initials in your chest for
the crows to see!

HERKIMER
Listen to the sergeant Men. Form
and fight in twos. (to Varick)
Tell Arnold we are through. Half
the 800 I brought are dead,
wounded -- missing in the woods.
Tell him the Mohawks are furious
with Burgoyne. He promised them
easy times. Now their best
warriors are dead here or
bloodied by their own Oneidas.
Chief Joseph Brandt is the only
force holding them to their
Devil's bargain.

Betrayal

Young Herkimer arrives and places grass stuffed in his shirt as a pillow for his father.

He rises and turns as Varick and Sullivan prepare to depart.

>YOUNG HERKIMER
>Richard... I'm sorry. Your foster father -- the Reverend -- is a good -

>VARICK
>We are all torn nine ways by this unholy war Young Herkimer. Take good care of your father. And yourself. I will look for you in better times.

DISSOLVE TO: EXT. WOODS NEAR ORISKANY CREEK - DAY

Sullivan guides Varick away from the battle as the rain stops and the dark clouds lift.

He looks back to see a militia man beside a tree fire and start to reload.

A Mohawk with his tomahawk raised charges.

The militia man's partner steps from behind the tree and shoots the Mohawk who falls almost on top of them.

Varick recoils, turns, and hurries to catch up.

A Screenplay

MOVE TO:

EXT. WOODS NEAR PITT TAVERN LATE AFTERNOON

Sullivan and Varick are riding side by side on a wide path.

                SULLIVAN
... and you seriously believe that John Adams wants to rub elbows with the likes of me. He writes to the newspapers condemning the unwashed masses who hunger for power and privilege. I hunger for power and privilege -- and don't wash excessively. But I respect Adams who doesn't want me to have what there might not be more than enough of for him and his. I respect him too for getting selfish madmen such as Arnold to do his killing and dying.

                VARICK
If you are not an outright traitor you must be a trimmer. You sound like my foster brother Joseph who serves with Sir William Howe in New York City.

                SULLIVAN
You are the only one I know, Old Varick, whom I suspect of terminal insanity. You actually breathe words like duty, honor, patriotism. You have company in a few men, Tom Paine, Sam Adams. At least Sam hopes to get his

British debts abolished. You and
Paine could struggle on for
years without realizing a
haypenny and be wildly blissful.
How were you formed Varick? And
where can I find more men like
you ready to die for a fancy?

                VARICK
You disgust me!

               SULLIVAN
And you amuse me. I shall --
Down! Quiet. Your life on it.

Sullivan pushes Varick from his saddle.

He holds his hand over Varick's mouth as they thrash on the ground.

Footsteps are heard and a woman's voice which Varick recognizes as Jane McCrea's.

                  JANE
I am sad that Mother and Father
and my brothers won't see me wed
at Albany. My... friend Richard
Varick too.

There is no answer.

Varick shakes his head back and forth and struggles to loosen Sullivan's grip on his mouth; he stops as he sees Principal and Second Runner walking ahead of Jane.

Sullivan whispers.

A Screenplay

> SULLIVAN
> She is not a prisoner. She is not bound. They are guiding her.

> VARICK
> I must talk to her. I know these Indians. They were at the McCrae farm with Hon Yost. I must talk to Jane.

> SULLIVAN
> They are in the woods now and they wear paint -- not the same Indians you knew. There must be others. There is no Hon Yost now.

> JANE
> Are you married Principal?

Principal turns momentarily as if to speak but moves on without a word.

Second Runner drops back.

SECOND RUNNER Principal. Handsome Lake. Marry.

> JANE
> What a beautiful name. (calls)
> Do you and Handsome Lake have children?

Principal without answering considers the question.

EXT. RIVER BY MOHAWK LONGHOUSES - DAY

Betrayal

Principal watches his stocky black-haired wife Handsome Lake gently washing his young son in the river.

BACK TO SCENE

                JANE
    Principal, can you hear me?

Jane looks at Second Runner who is non-committal.

              VARICK
    I must speak to her. I can't
    leave things the way –

Second Runner stops and listens.

He starts to slowly retrace his steps.

Sullivan eases Varick away.

                      MOVE TO:

EXT./INT. WILLIAM PITT TAVERN – NIGHT

Sullivan is hitching his horse to a post as Varick rides up and dismounts quickly.

              SULLIVAN
    It might be best, Lieutenant
    Varick, to have a good wash and
    listen awhile before we seek
    volunteers. This place attracts
    a motley crew and patience can
    pay dividends that haste—

A Screenplay

              VARICK
   Patience! Brave men like
   Herkimer risk their lives and
   you caution patience. We count
   ourselves lucky to have 30,000
   men in the field when we should
   have 300,000. These tavern
   loafers must rise to their duty.
   I will mind them of it.

Sullivan sighs as mud-smeared, bedraggled Varick charges past him into the tavern.

JONATHAN PAULUS is reading aloud from rebel newspapers at the bar.

Men are playing cards, throwing darts, drinking and shouting.

Several tavern patrons, a barmaid, and the INNKEEPER are listening and chuckling at Paulus's comments.

              PAULUS
   This from The Pennsylvania
   Gazette: 'We have lately learned
   from an exchanged prisoner of
   the Christian proclivities of
   that kind general, Swagger
   Burgoyne. The great one
   proclaims to his allies the
   savage Indians that they should
   not attack the old, the infirm,
   women, children, or Tories, and
   they must only scalp dead
   rebels, not wounded ones. Edmund
   Burke told Parliament this is
   akin to loosing lions from the
   Tower of London Zoo and asking

them to eat only members of the
Opposition.'

As all laugh a bedraggled Varick strides in
purposefully.

>   PAULUS
> Plain to see we have our own
> homegrown fools.

>   VARICK
> I am Lieutenant Richard Varick
> of the Continental American Army
> serving with General Benedict
> Arnold.

>   PAULUS
> Most impressive. I am Jonathan
> Paulus of the William Pitt
> Tavern regulars. I am served
> here at the Innkeeper's
> pleasure.

>   VARICK
> I have come to seek republicans.
> Men of action who would protect
> their country in its fight for
> independence. I come for
> patriots, men of gumption

Paulus holds up a recruiting poster.

>   PAULUS
> We have your poster: 'A few
> happy years viewing different
> parts of this beautiful
> country.' Then we return home in
> glory? With laurels? Pockets
> full of money?

A Screenplay

> VARICK
> Most importantly we will have shown the world that we are a new nation, proud and—

> PAULUS
> Help us with the arithmetic, Kind Sir. We get a twelve-dollar bonus to join the raggedy Continental Army for a few happy years of running from the British or we get a fifty-dollar bonus to sign with our Mohawk Valley militia for three months here amidst food and shelter aplenty. Is this not a conundrum, Men? What are we to do?

> DRUNKEN FARMER
> Tar and feather the bastard!

> VARICK
> Sergeant, (pointing to Paulus) that man is seditious! Arrest him!
> All games stop as the patrons protest loudly and surround Varick and Paulus.

> VARICK
> I will not have treason spoken the same day that valiant men have died at Oriskany Creek opposing the forces of—

Betrayal

> SULLIVAN
> Lieutenant. Sir, these men consider it treason to suppress their opinions. (Moves between Varick and patrons.) All right, Men, the lieutenant is a bit dazed from battle exertions. In his better moments, he would stand us all a round of rum punch so let me order it for him. Innkeeper! Your biggest bowls, your best rum.

The patrons shout approval and murmur about Oriskany and Herkimer as they crowd the bar.

One repeats 'What are we to do?' He and his companion laugh heartily.

> VARICK
> You need not lie for me, Sergeant. You are risking court martial.

> SULLIVAN
> Sir, be a little easy. You are risking death with fringe men here who change coats as the wind shifts. They would shoot you in the back and sell your carcass to whichever army pays a trifle. Our best choice when they are properly rumored up is to get them singing Yankee Doodle Dandy. Perhaps a dozen will sign on for Fort Stanwix.

A Screenplay

> VARICK
> A dozen? We can not disappoint General Arnold. If Washington can not send Morgan's rifles, we must raise hundreds. We -- Sullivan... I don't have money enough to pay for the punch!

> SULLIVAN
> Of course you don't, but I love the grand gesture of it all. You keep on, Old Varick, and you'll be another Benedict Arnold. God save Congress! Up the Republic!

> INNKEEPER
> The punch! Who pays for the punch?

> SULLIVAN
> Add two piping hot baths and your biggest bed for the night and send your account to General Arnold. His word is as good as gold.

> INNKEEPER
> Arnold! He owes me yet for a visit last year. You'll swab out my stables.

Sullivan drains a punch bowl.

He pulls Varick from the bar where he is expounding.

Sullivan pushes the reluctant Varick out to his horse. Varick mounts while protesting.

Betrayal

> VARICK
> What is this unseemly rush?

> SULLIVAN
> Best we forego enlistments tonight, Sir, and move on. I prefer sleeping under the stars to shoveling shit. I accept your wisdom -- a dozen men is a drop in the ocean. (He slaps Varick's horse's rump.) A little patience next time?

The innkeeper rushes out with a musket and aims it at Varick's back.

Sullivan steps from the shadows and discharges his pistol next to the innkeeper who jumps, fires in the air, and drops his musket.

Sullivan mounts and calls into the inn.

> SULLIVAN
> Fire in the stables! Not a bad punch, Innkeeper. We'll spread your fame.

Patrons rush out jostling the innkeeper who searches for his musket as Sullivan saunters off.

> DRUNKEN FARMER
> Tar and feather the bastards!

CUT TO:

EXT. HILL NEAR ARNOLD'S CAMP - DAY

A Screenplay

Hon Yost is doing somersaults, playing a few notes on his Jew's harp, and tumbling down the hill again.

His brother Nicholas looks from him to the crest of the hill where Mrs. Yost is trying to catch her breath.

                NICHOLAS
    Wait up Hon! Mother is winded.
    Hon Yost stops, pulls a spyglass
    from his shirt, and trains it on
    Arnold's camp.

                HON YOST
    I must report to General St.
    Leger now. He offers me a pound
    sterling for good information.
    Time is money he says to me.
    (Sings.) Time is money he says
    to me.

Hon Yost tucks his spyglass in his shirt and does a somersault.

As he lands on his feet a lasso encircles him. He turns to see Piggott smiling at him.

Nimbly he moves toward Piggott, letting the rope slacken, and quickly steps out of it and runs away.

                PIGGOTT
    Not too fast Friend Yost.

                NICHOLAS
    Hon!

Betrayal

Hon Yost turns back to see Piggott fingering the blade of his huge hunting knife as he stands beside Mrs. Yost who says nothing but looks stricken.

                NICHOLAS
   You would not slay a woman -- a
   mother -our mother.
                PIGGOTT
   My blade has no preference, no
   partialities. All sizes, all
   sexes.

                NICHOLAS
   Come back Hon.

Piggott offers Mrs. Yost his arm which she takes gingerly.

                PIGGOTT
   Would a hot cup of tea suit you,
   Mother Yost?

Piggott heads down the hill to Arnold's camp, slowing down so Mrs. Yost can keep up with him.

Nicholas follows closely.

Hon Yost tags after, playing hide-and-seek from tree to tree.

(End of third Hour p. 110)

                                      CUT TO:

EXT. SMALL HILL NEAR ARNOLD'S CAMP - AFTERNOON

A Screenplay

As Varick and Sullivan approach on horseback, Varick looks up to see the Abnaki Indian sachem NATANIS sitting cross-legged on a rock staring just above and beyond the two riders, holding something in his lap and chanting.

Varick leaps sideways to push Sullivan to the ground.

              VARICK
  Down!

Sullivan reins his horse sharply.

Varick flies past to land heavily on the ground. Natanis rises. He is holding prayer beads.

              SULLIVAN
  Natanis.

              NATANIS
  Sully -- van... this is an
  officer?

              SULLIVAN
  A Varick. Lieuenant Richard
  Varick from the Mohawk Valley.
  Serving your friend Benedict
  Arnold the Dark Eagle.

              NATANIS
  Do my cousins the Mohawks run
  before in dread of Lieutenant
  Var-reek?

Betrayal

> SULLIVAN
> Not quite yet. He is a mite shy of The Dark Eagle's fame. All right there, Lieutenant Varick? Thank you for saving my life. This desperate savage is Natanis, honored wise man of the Abnakis who saved our bacon in the great Maine woods on our way to Quebec.

Varick brushes himself off and limps toward Arnold's camp, leading his horse.

Sullivan dismounts and holds his horse's reins for Natanis to mount.

They chat as they follow Varick to Arnold's camp.

> SULLIVAN
> How is Roaring Falls?

> NATANIS
> Loud... your woman in Eyer-lan?

> SULLIVAN
> Mercifully soft -- at least on the written page if I send her money for the babes.

> NATANIS
> Money. The Dark Eagle has it?

Sullivan shrugs to indicate that he does not know.

A Screenplay

      NATANIS
 Sully-van is loyal to Mad
 Arnold.

Sullivan shrugs.

EXT. TRAIL CROSSING NEAR ARNOLD'S CAMP -
DUSK

Varick and Sullivan and Natanis start
through the crossing when they hear a
strange hollow-sounding voice coming from
the woods nearby.

      PIGGOTT
 Why has the great sachem of the
 Abnakis come to Arnold's woods?

      NATANIS
 Pigg -- Ott!
 A smiling Hon Yost dances
 happily into the crosing ahead
 of Piggott who discards a hollow
 trunk to grip Natanis's arm.

      PIGGOTT
 You join us?

      NATANIS
 No, Friend. Joseph Brandt calls
 me to Stanwix to read signs for
 his Mohawk warriors who bleed
 from British lies and Oneida
 hatchets.

      PIGGOTT
 You will stay out of the
 crossfire?

Betrayal

NATANIS
I will try. My brother is hostage in the Mohawk longhouses. If I serve Joseph Brandt well, my brother returns home with me.

PIGGOTT
If you were to escort the Yosts, Sergeant Sullivan, I would consider it a privilege to entertain our honored visitor.

SULLIVAN
A capital idea. Lieutenant Varick and I will take the desperado in while we report to General Arnold. You may share your collection of scalps with our esteemed guest and your supply of dandelion wine. Please refrain, however, from discussing the laws of nations any earlier than the twelfth century.

NATANIS
Pigg -- ott [still] has many words.

SULLIVAN
And legal issues to rock the world.

A Screenplay

                    PIGGOTT
Would you please see that Mrs.
Yost gets a nice cup of
Cambridge tea.

                                    CUT TO:

EXT. ARNOLD'S HEADQUARTERS TENT – NIGHT

Arnold is writing and folding passes at a
furious clip. Sullivan and Varick approach,
stop, wait.
They signal the Yosts to stay where they
are.

Hon Yost takes his Jew's harp from his
pocket, shakes dirt from it, and begins to
play.

                    ARNOLD
Report.

                    VARICK
We went to Oriskany Creek first
and later to the William Pitt
tavern but it seems

                    ARNOLD
Sergeant.

                    SULLIVAN
Herkimer's mauled and no musket
men. Natanis looks for money en
route to Joseph Brant at
Stanwix. Piggott entertains him.
We've caught a strange bird,
half cracked, spying on the
camp.

Betrayal

> ARNOLD
>
> The musician.

> VARICK
>
> Hon Yost is from the Valley, Sir. Neither side can trust him but he has delivered messages and means no real harm. The Mohawks revere him as closer to their gods. He might help at Fort Stanwix if he can be persuaded to -

> ARNOLD
>
> Build a gallows, Sergeant, very slowly. Keep all parties separate. Let them imagine alone.

> SULLIVAN
>
> Sir!

> VARICK
>
> The Six Nations consider Fort Stanwix a special place because it was supposed to be the stopping line for settlement. It hasn't proven to be so the Mohawks with St. Leger are not sure if it is a holy or a cursed place. They -

> ARNOLD
>
> I will listen to your ideas Lieutenant as we ride to meet one of my agents.

EXT. A CLEARING NEAR ARNOLD'S CAMP - MIDNIGHT

A Screenplay

Varick and Franks watch JOSHUA HETT SMITH as he skulks toward Arnold carrying a heavy rounded bag.

He looks around as if he may be followed.

Arnold at a distance is pacing and studying the moon and skies and the waterfall in the background while fidgeting with his hands.

>   VARICK
> Why are we here? At midnight?
>   FRANKS
> Because Joshua Hett Smith can not bring himself to buy his passes to New York City in broad daylight as the rest of Arnold's less imaginative associates do. The hour and circumstances appeal to Our Little General's dramatic side also.

>   VARICK
> Why would General Arnold sell –

Arnold hears something, turns quickly and draws his sword.

Smith jumps back and drops his bag. Coins spill on the ground.

Arnold frowns as Smith scurries to pick up the coins and return them to the bag.

>   VARICK
> Oh... for money.

Betrayal

                    FRANKS
Privileges of rank. If I were in
Arnold's position, I would
employ a special Quartermaster
for Dubious Passes and rake in
specie by the barrelful.

                    VARICK
That man Smith man looks
especially scruffy and
suspicious -- like a varlet.

                    FRANKS
A what? Arnold has made good use
of such and General Washington
is the master at it. Good George
treats them like visiting
plenipotentiaries: 'Fancy some
sherry, Mister Scum?'
Occasionally it pays dividends.

                    VARICK
Does General Arnold believe that
Smith truly is a double agent?

                    FRANKS
Smith keeps a foot in both camps
but everyone in the state of New
York knows that he and his
brother are with the King. Our
Little General chooses to ignore
this or feigns ignorance.

Smith comes away from Arnold carrying
pieces of paper which he scans and folds.

A Screenplay

He looks around and tucks the passes in his vest.

          FRANKS
Ah, he has his passes. The City of New York is his oyster.

Smith cautiously approaches en route to his horse.

          FRANKS
How came you here, Mister Smith? Smith looks around as if checking for a trap.

          JOSHUA HETT SMITH
My faithful steed George carried me.

          FRANKS
Could that George be for George the Third or George Washington?

          JOSHUA HETT SMITH
It could.

          FRANKS
Did you come from the party above in Skenesboro or those below in Albany?

          JOSHUA HETT SMITH
Yesss.

          FRANKS
Where were you yesterday?

          JOSHUA HETT SMITH
Partly in bed.

Betrayal

               FRANKS
Which part?

          JOSHUA HETT SMITH
Sir? In bed, partly. I strive to spend a soft nine or ten hours in bed to promote my health. I am, did you know, poor sickly.

               FRANKS
Ahh, that explains it.

          JOSHUA HETT SMITH
Explains which?
               FRANKS
Yessss.

Franks nods his head knowingly as if digesting new information.

Smith, looking alarmed, skulks off.

               VARICK
I believe in fair trials and all that, but you know and I know that men such as that are guilty of -

               FRANKS
Looking scruffy and suspicious? Acting hopelessly treacherous? Totally incompetent?

               VARICK
You understand perfectly what I intend.

A Screenplay

            FRANKS
I do indeed, Your Worship. You intend to be judge, jury, and star witness. And executioner in the bargain. An English lord of the manor.

            VARICK
You confuse my words!

            FRANKS
Or clarify them.

            VARICK
Franks! You're getting dangerously close to insulting my integrity.

            FRANKS
I would not have you put to the trouble of a duel, Sir Richard. Just hang me next the nearest -- uh -- varlet.

Arnold finishes stuffing his saddle bags as he calls.

            ARNOLD
Major! We ride.

            FRANKS
  General!

As Franks and Varick hurry to their horses, Arnold rides by them.

Franks leaps on his horse and follows closely.

Varick hesitates, scribbles in his journal, mounts, and follows.

                              CUT TO:

EXT. MOHAWK VALLEY WOODS - LATE AFTERNOON

Principal and Second Runner and Jane walk in single file.

Jane tries to hear what Second Runner is saying to Principal and Principal's responses.

              SECOND RUNNER
  I will not allow it.

Principal looks back but says nothing.

              SECOND RUNNER
  Handsome Lake is your wife, the mother of your son.

              PRINCIPAL
  I know this.

              JANE
  Is Principal homesick? Does he miss his wife?

Second Runner hears Jane but does not answer.

                              CUT TO:

INT. ARNOLD'S HQ TENT - AFTERNOON

Arnold is sorting correspondence, balling some pages up and throwing them into the fire, meticulously straightening piles.

A Screenplay

Varick is writing amidst a messy pile of correspondence, watching Arnold and speaking to his back.

>ARNOLD
>I call her 'Girl' and she answers to it. In tender moments I refer to her as 'Young Girl' or 'Missy.'

>VARICK
>She just folded her tent, packed her mule, and left?

>ARNOLD
>That is her prerogative.

>VARICK
>I did not get to say goodbye to her. Her name is Alinda Breitvogel. It means 'bright bird'.

>ARNOLD
>That's lovely, Lieutenant Varick. Shall we dance? Or did you have a notion to help me with my correspondence this afternoon?

>VARICK
>I am just finishing this significant amount of morning letters, Sir.

Betrayal

> ARNOLD
> Fine, Lieutenant. Perhaps we'll exceed that this afternoon..

Sullivan calls from outside the tent.

> SULLIVAN
> General Arnold, Sir!

> ARNOLD
> Yes, Sergeant? Come ahead.
> Sullivan enters and salutes smartly. Arnold is reading a letter.

> SULLIVAN
> Natanis is smoking great pipes with Piggott. We hear that General Charles Lee is headed this way with Congress's loyalty oaths for all to sign.

> ARNOLD
> we will welcome Charles Lee as a highly respected general with full turnout. He must carry General Washington's answer to my request for Morgan's company. Keep Natanis away from me a while more until I have my plan full ready.

> SULLIVAN
> Sir!

Sullivan leaves.

Arnold lays the letter down and paces behind Varick who sits with pen poised above a blank piece of paper.

A Screenplay

As Arnold's voice rises, the tone changes from neutral to harsh.

> ARNOLD
> I had had high hopes Lieutenant Varick that you would soon become that most valuable of secretaries who could read my correspondence and draft a reply as personal as if I had written it myself. Please read these few lines you wrote to my sister Hannah -- Hannah, the loving sister who cares for my children since their mother died, my rock, my steadfast companion in every crisis.

Varick picks up the letter gingerly and reads in a soft voice.

> VARICK
> 'I too was affected by Father's lingering illness and my painful removal from Canterbury School-

> ARNOLD
> Louder please, Mister Varick.

> VARICK
> 'My painful removal from Canterbury School' -- that must have been difficult in the extreme for your entire family, General. When my father came wounded home from the French and Indian wars he lay in the living room for three years before—

Betrayal

ARNOLD
My father's illness was that of a drunkard. I do not need to remind... my sister insists on sharing every anniversary painful or not -- let us look at my accounts. Henceforth I will write to Hannah and the boys. Is there nothing but old bills left? Well then, let us attack them.

VARICK
There is one from the innkeeper at William Pitt Tavern that seems immediate. He threatens to engage an attorney unless it is paid forthwith.

ARNOLD
How much does he claim is owed him?

VARICK
One hundred and thirty-seven pounds, seven shillings, sixpence.

ARNOLD
In my master log, Lieutenant, enter two hundred pounds, seven shillings, sixpence. No -- make that two hundred and one. They seem to accept odd numbers better than even.

A Screenplay

> VARICK
> What shall I enter for the extra sixty-some pounds, Sir?

> ARNOLD
> Just what the bill lists, Mister Varick. I will not trouble Congress with a recitation of incidental expenses I incurred with serving wenches and stable grooms and -- burn that bill. And any subsequent ones from the same source.

> VARICK
> Burn the bill, Sir? But what proof will you have that—

> ARNOLD
> Proof? My word is proof enough! I will not enter into petty squabbles with soft men who sit all day and drone on about freedom. I fight for liberty but I will not haggle -- I gave them meticulous accounts for Quebec and they have paid not a haypenny. They have abused me. Nor would they accept that I grounded my flagship and set it afire at Valcour Island without pausing to gather up my records. Should I have waited for the British to climb aboard!

Arnold pulls several bills from his lockbox and tears and flings them.

Betrayal

He closes his eyes and stands still, breathing heavily. Franks calls from outside the tent.

          FRANKS
  General Arnold, you wished to
  know when your special shipment
  arrived.

          ARNOLD
  Thank you, Major Franks.

Varick speaks very softly.

          VARICK
  Sir.

          ARNOLD
  Lieutenant.

          VARICK
  I can not enter the sum you wish
  in your master log and I can not
  burn this document.

          ARNOLD
  Document? A padded bill from a
  thief of a tavern owner is now
  become a document. Since when
  did you -- you do realize that I
  could have you court-martialed
  for disobeying a clear directive
  from me, do you not?

          VARICK
  Sir, I do.

A Screenplay

              ARNOLD
You are a fool, Mister Varick, in the ways of the world. Do you not think that our great and good General Washington estimates -- but -- you have a spine. Enough paperwork. I've developed a savage thirst so I must walk a mile before I slake it. Good evening, Lieutenant Varick.

Varick rises and bumps into the table as Arnold bolts for his hat and starts out of the tent.

He pauses.

              ARNOLD
Keep with you two thoughts, Lieutenant Richard Varick. One. In another context, another moment, another mood, you would be in chains now. Two. What transpires between us is not to be shared with anyone. Anyone!

Varick nods as Arnold marches from the tent. Varick begins to pick up the torn pieces of paper. He stops to read one.

     INSERT: Varick READS:
Aaron Selyu, Shipbuilder, Newburyport, Massachusetts
Valcour Island Services: 77 pounds September 1776

Varick searches in his duffel bag until he finds the journal given him by Sullivan.

Betrayal

He writes a quick note in it, then scans several pieces of paper.

He stops to read one from Washington to Arnold.

> INSERT
> We HEAR Washington's voice as Varick READS:
>
> WASHINGTON
> August 7, 1777 Dear General Arnold, My spymaster has intercepted a message in your handwriting signed 'Moncks.' I recognized your hand and allowed your agent to pass through the lines, but it might be prudent to employ another. Said Joshua Hett Smith is developing a reputation as dubious at best. There are among my men those who swear he is a British agent and would disembowel him given half the chance. Good fortune in your fishing expeditions. Your humble servant, G. Washington

Varick re-opens his journal, scribbles quickly in it, closes it, and looks around furtively.

He replaces the two pieces of paper and tidies the rest.

                                    CUT TO:

EXT. TRAIL LEADING TO THE TOP OF A HILL - EVENING

A Screenplay

Principal ranges ahead.

Jane struggles to come close enough to Second Runner to speak.

> **JANE**
> Second Runner, does Principal dislike me? He looks at me in the strangest way sometimes. Other times, he does not respond or ignores me completely. Have I said or done something to offend him?

Second Runner hesitates as if about to speak; instead, he charges ahead.

> **JANE**
> Second Runner?

> **SECOND RUNNER**
> Come.

EXT. ROAD LEADING TO ARNOLD'S CAMP - MORNING

Hundreds of militia are in two rows facing each other forming a lane.

At the front of the lane flowers cover the ground.

At the end of the lane Arnold and Franks and Varick and the other officers are waiting on horseback.

All are relaxing or slouching except Arnold who stares straight ahead and Sullivan who stands at attention beside Arnold.

Betrayal

In the near background Piggott gathers and smells flowers as Natanis watches.

Off to the side a large, loose, makeshift band is getting ready

           VARICK
Why so much ceremony for one general? Would we do any more if George Washington came to visit?

           SULLIVAN
There you have it, Lieutenant. Sharp as a tack. You begin to see the method in General Lee's madness. He personally presides while thousands sign loyalty oaths. To whom will they feel a loyalty should Congress decide –

           VARICK
You read too much into what is assuredly an oppressive task for a battle-tested veteran like General Lee.

           FRANKS
Mind your P's and Q's. That cloud of dust approaching is, I'll wager, our fearless macaroni General Charles Lee.

They all watch as GENERAL CHARLES LEE and a pack of dogs trot into view. He is tall and angular and rumpled.

Behind him is a servant.

A Screenplay

Bringing up the rear is a soiled but vaguely pretty woman in plain worn clothes with a shiny new red ribbon in her hair.

Lee holds his favorite beribboned dog Mirabelle on his saddle.

Varick and Sullivan watch Lee waving his hat to the cheering soldiers.

> SULLIVAN
> Does he strike you as oppressed, Sir?

A few soldiers attempt to pet Lee's dogs but are rebuffed by snarls.

> CHARLES LEE
> Get away from my animals!

> NATANIS
> Boiling Water's dogs share his humors.

> SULLIVAN
> And I have it from impeccable sources that General Lee has not signed his own loyalty oath.

> VARICK
> Are you indulging in gossip again, Sergeant?

> SULLIVAN
> I purely hope so. Sir. In this instance I have it direct from Piggott's cousin, by way of Piggott of course, that gossip

and gospel truth are one and
the same. I would bet General
Arnold knows.

Without turning Arnold responds.

> ARNOLD
> Yes.

> VARICK
> He has not signed?

> ARNOLD
> Yes.

> VARICK
> How can he ask others to do so
> when he himself hesitates?

> SULLIVAN
> Years of practice on
> battlefields ordering soldiers
> to go where he will not lead.

> ARNOLD
> Enough... Sergeant.

> SULLIVAN
> Tennn -- shun!

The militia try to look militarily sharp as
they come to attention.

> SULLIVAN
> Preeezent harms!

The militia hold their rifles in front of
them more or less correctly.

A Screenplay

Arnold and the officers and Sullivan hold their salutes. Lee does not return his until he is very close.

>   CHARLES LEE
>   Arnold! How kind to receive me
>   so warmly. Not at all necessary.
>   I come merely to carry out
>   Congress's wishes to allow all
>   loyal Patriots –

Lee is startled when the makeshift band breaks into its first song, a loud, rough version of "Yankee Doodle Dandy."

Arnold forces a smile and gestures to tell Lee that the band means well.

He rides with Lee toward camp.

Franks and the young officers follow.

Sullivan dismisses the militia, but indicates that the band is to continue playing.

Varick and Sullivan watch the militia run in every direction.

>   VARICK
>   Truly, why is he here?

>   SULLIVAN
>   To spy for Gates, to spy for
>   Congress, to position himself if
>   Washington slips, to lecture
>   Arnold on tactics best left in
>   Europe, to indulge in pleasures
>   of the flesh –

Betrayal

                    VARICK
          I should not have asked.

                                        CUT TO:

EXT. BURGOYNE'S CAMP AT SKENESBORO - DAY

General Burgoyne is waving encouragement and bowing occasionally to COLONEL FREIDRICH BAUM who is readying his Hessian troops to march into Vermont.

Two military bands are practicing martial tunes. MRS. BAUM and her children applaud each new song. Soldiers are adjusting each other's gear.

Colonel Phillips and Philip Skene stand on either side of Burgoyne.

Phillips shouts over the loud, erratic music with mounting annoyance to Skene who responds only to Burgoyne.

                    PHILLIPS
          Might Colonel Baum's Hessians
          travel more quickly without
          those huge boots they are
          wearing Mister -

Burgoyne glances at Phillips.

                    PHILLIPS
          Major Skene.

                    SKENE
          Colonel Baum assures us Dear
          General Burgoyne that his men
          are more comfortable marching in

their high dress boots.

> PHILLIPS
> Might this lightning raid on Bennington be more lightning-like and less like unhorsed ancient knights in armor if the dragoons trimmed their hundred-pound packs and left those heavy metal helmets in camp?

> SKENE
> Colonel Baum says -- begging The General's indulgence -- that his men feel more protected carrying full issue and wearing their helmets. We will have Indians and local Loyalists for the light skirmishing.

> PHILLIPS
> You are quite certain the loyal population will awake and rise?

> SKENE
> The dragoons intend to return mounted on the rebels' finest horses.

> BURGOYNE
> Quite. With the horses and food and gunpowder the good colonel siezes at Bennington we will have the provision needed to join forces with Howe at Albany.

> PHILLIPS
> The rebels may be a trifle slow-

witted but might not there be
one officer amongst them who
notices the noise produced by
two entire military bands
approaching -- drums beating -

          SKENE
A question of morale, Your
Eminence.

          PHILLIPS
-- cymbals clashing? Might not?
          SKENE
Colonel Baum believes his men
march more spiritedly with
martial music playing. We shall
of course caution the strictest
silences as we approach the
rebel storehouses in Bennington.
Not to worry Honored Warrior.
Hundreds of Tories will join us
en route and Baum's Hessians
under our advisement will acquit
themselves well in the Vermont
woods.

          PHILLIPS
Should they not die en route of
heat exhaustion.

Baum turns to salute Burgoyne.

          SKENE
We must be off. Look for us in a
week or less Dear General and
prepare to feast on the fresh
victuals we bring. Coming
Colonel.

A Screenplay

Skene signals a black bewigged liveried servant who struggles to place Skene's huge heavy chest in a waiting carriage.

Skene rushes to pull the chest, which the servant has almost wrestled into the carriage, onto the ground.

He strikes the servant with his riding crop.

            SKENE
   You oaf. There is only one way
   to place a trunk in a carriage -
   - from the left side you booby.

Skene and Baum smile and bow to each other and talk with hand signals.

They turn and bow not quite in unison to Burgoyne.

He tries to cheerfully return the enthusiastic salutes of Skene and Baum as the troops parade in review.

Burgoyne grimaces at the discordance of both military bands playing simultaneously.

Skene gestures toward Baum and his men who march off smartly. Skene smiles and nods.

He offhandedly strikes his servant again as he climbs into the carriage.

Burgoyne nods and forces a smile.

Phillips looks troubled.

Betrayal

                                        CUT TO:

EXT. SWIMMING HOLE IN A QUARRY NEAR
ARNOLD'S CAMP - DAY

Arnold with his coat open is pacing around
a map table which Franks in full uniform
leans over.

Richard Varick, his coat off and his shirt
open, meticulously copies a large map of
the Fort Stanwix area, pausing frequently
to glance at Arnold.

Sullivan is naked to the waist, lying on a
blanket sunning himself.

Piggott is standing in the water, his pants
rolled up, questioning Sullivan and
carefully writing down his answers.

In the background soldiers jump ump and
dive friom the cliffs.

A very fat soldier cannonballs from a high
ledge drenching Sullivan and Piggott.

Sullivan sits up and scowls. Piggott
remains in position unperturbed.

                    PIGGOTT
          Is it your position, Sergeant
          Sullivan, that when you threw my
          trunk onto the road leaving Fort
          Ticonderoga you were not aware
          that valuable legal documents
          resided within the trunk?

Sullivan moves his head up and down.

A Screenplay

> PIGGOTT
> Could you please, for the
> record, utter speech.

> SULLIVAN
> Yes, Corporal Piggott, that is
> my official position.

Piggott nods his head and then tilts it as he adopts a crafty look.

> PIGGOTT
> What then did you think was in
> that trunk?

> SULLIVAN
> A mess of silly scribblings.

> PIGGOTT
> A what?

> ARNOLD
> Lieutenant Varick, you need not
> watch my every move. As soon as
> General Lee passes on General
> Washington's reply, I shall
> share it with you.

From the hill above the high screechy voice of General Charles Lee is heard.

> CHARLES LEE
> Piggotttt!

Piggott comes to strict attention.

His dog Old Lump comes waddling down the hill at top speed.

Betrayal

                    PIGGOTT
Suh!

Lee runs and stumbles down the hill to the water's edge.

He holds three dogs on leashes, two Greyhounds and his poodle Mirabelle which is immaculately groomed and beribboned. Lee is dressed in a filthy, rumpled, expensive dressing gown and ornate slippers. His hair is stringy and his gestures wild.

                    CHARLES LEE
    Pregnant, Piggott, pregnant!

                    PIGGOTT
    Sir, no sir!

                    CHARLES LEE
    That filthy beast of yours has gone and mounted my Mirabelle. She could be PREGNAANNNT! I caught him in the act.

                    PIGGOTT
    Sir. Congratulations! Don't they make a fine pair.

Lee wrestles a pistol out of his dressing gown pocket and aims it at Piggott's crotch.

                    CHARLES LEE
    You'll never be a proud father.

Piggott dives into the water. Sullivan wrestles with General Lee.

A Screenplay

As Sullivan tries to disarm the enraged, squirming Lee, Piggott surfaces to ask a new series of questions.

            PIGGOTT
    Am I officially on duty,
    Sergeant Sullivan? Have I been
    attacked while in performance of
    my duty? Would any military
    court see –

Sullivan and Lee continue to wrestle as they roll toward the water.

Sullivan indicates to Varick with a jerk of his thumb that he should get Piggott out of the area.

            VARICK
    Corporal Piggott! General Arnold
    wants you to reconnoiter west of
    here. Right now! Indians.
    Tories. Redcoats. Just count
    them. Don't attack.

Piggott nods and gets down on his knees to ask his next question of Sullivan.

Lee rolls on top of Sullivan, chokes him, and reaches in vain to grab Piggott.

            PIGGOTT
    Do you recommend a written
    report, Sergeant, or shall I—

            SULLIVAN
    Written -- in a clear hand – no
    embellishments. Go Piggott. Now!
    (With difficulty under his

breath) Or I shall -- use
General Lee's gun to -- finish -

           PIGGOTT
You may place your rigid trust
in me Serg

Varick and Franks and a few of the
young officers pull Piggott away from
Lee, who is still trying to grasp him,
and put Piggott on a horse. Arnold slaps
the horse's rump.

Varick helps Sullivan disarm the frenetic
squirming Lee as Piggott gallops off.

Sullivan and Lee roll into the water and
stop flailing.

          SULLIVAN
God speed, My Corporal!

           ARNOLD
I apologize General Lee on
behalf of my entire company for
this wretched crime. I will have
Piggott—

          SULLIVAN
Not -- Corporal Piggott. Sir.
It was me. I was in my cups
when word came from the old
country that my favorite hunting
dog, uh, Fox For Sure -- had
gone to meet his maker. I was
telling Old Lump about it, not
paying enough mind to his rope.
He escaped and, despite stern
injunctions from Corporal

A Screenplay

> Piggott, proffered his
> attentions to General Lee's
> beautiful Mirabelle. The rest
> you know.

>   ARNOLD
> This is a disgrace Sullivan. You
> are no longer a sergeant in
> my army. General Lee, do you
> wish him hung? Dereliction of
> duty?

Lee is startled by the suggestion. Then he reconsiders it. He stands in shallow water and shakes himself.

>   CHARLES LEE
> Perhaps it would teach this
> rabble a little respect for
> property. I am more concerned
> that Corporal Piggott not think
> me an unfair leader of men.

>   SULLIVAN
> No fear of that, Your Eminence.

Arnold glances at Sullivan to shut him up.

>   CHARLES LEE
> I did not realize that Sullivan
> was the dens ex machina in the
> whole affair. Certainly explains
> his exertions to restrain me.
> Not hung, Arnold, just a
> thousand lashes to teach the
> lads while showing mercy. Not
> hung. This time.

Arnold glances at Sullivan and nods toward

Lee.

                   SULLIVAN
    Thank you, Sir. God grant my
    back serve as a manual of
    decorum for all misguided
    military and a testament to your
    saintly forbearance.

Arnold frowns at Sullivan to let him know that he is laying it on too thick.

                   SULLIVAN
    Bless you, General Lee, and all
    the animals in your household
    now and—

                   ARNOLD
    Sergeant of the guard!

A puzzled, fretful young militia man approaches tentatively and salutes awkwardly.

                   ARNOLD
    Take Sergeant -- no -- Private
    Sullivan to the whipping tree.

                   MILITIA MAN
    The which tree, Sir?

                   ARNOLD
    The whipping tree. where is the
    Sergeant of the Guard when I
    need him?

                   MILITIA MAN
    Sir, Sergeant Sullivan --
    Private Sullivan -- Mister

A Screenplay

>Sullivan is the Sergeant of the Guard. Sir.

The militia man fumbles with his weapon, hesitates, then salutes again.

>ARNOLD
>Take this -- this -- Sullivan to his tent and guard him closely.

The militia man does not know if he should go before or after Sullivan who is trying to keep from laughing.

Arnold suppresses a smile.

Sullivan silently directs the militia man to follow, then motions to him to close the distance.

Sullivan slumps as if totally dejected. Lump gets up and ambles over to Mirabelle.

>CHARLES LEE
>I must be off, General Arnold. I shall recount to General Gates how you enforce military discipline with alacrity. Would that a certain high personage had such decisiveness.

>ARNOLD
>You could not mean our Commander-inChief, could you General?

Lee looks about secretively. Arnold stares directly at him. Lee speaks in a loud whisper.

> CHARLES LEE
> The man could not command a corporal's guard.

> ARNOLD
> I beg to differ, Sir. There may be others more fearsome in the field but as for commanding deserved respect, I know no other who—

> CHARLES LEE
> Loyal of you to say so but we all know –

> ARNOLD
> Did General Washington send a message with you?

> CHARLES LEE
> He can let you have Daniel Morgan and twenty or thirty of his rifles for a brief time. Per usual, he keeps most of the veteran troops by him even though he is at a loss to employ them effectively.

> ARNOLD
> You're sure he said twenty or thirty?

> CHARLES LEE
> Something of that order. Thank you for your hospitality Arnold. God grant you victory in

> whatever it is you do in these
> wilds. I must visit Gates
> before I return to Albany.
> Never did I think I should
> consider that backward village
> as a haven of -- come Girls.
> General Gates, I am sure, has
> some choice tidbits -- for us
> all.

Lee picks up Mirabelle to get her away from Lump who is sniffing her.

Franks bows to Lee as he leaves to climb the hill. Arnold turns his back.

EXT. CLEARING AT TOP OF HILL - DUSK

Jane is seated looking out over the valley. Second Runner is touching his tomahawk.

Principal can not stand still.

> JANE
> I think I can see my home from
> here. No, I'm sure that I am
> just imagining it. Do we have
> far to go? Will we travel
> tonight?

Jane turns but Principal and Second Runner have disappeared into the woods.

She puzzles for a moment, then returns to contemplating.

> JANE
> (to herself) I hope Burton loves
> me in the years ahead as much as

Principal cares for Handsome Lake.

CUT TO:

EXT. GREEN NEAR ARNOLD'S HEADQUARTERS TENT - DAY
Fifty of Morgan's sharpshooters are practicing and roughhousing on the cleared green in front of Arnold's headquarters tent. Arnold is talking forcefully to Daniel Morgan as Varick stops reading a manual to listen and Sullivan tries to act preoccupied with the wicks of lamps.

                    ARNOLD
          You will note, Colonel Morgan,
          that Herkimer sent a message
          with an Oneida who betrayed
          him, Natanis has reason not
          to, but I would not overtrust
          him. He is indebted to Chief
          Joseph Brandt. Send two of your
          sharpshooters in the wake of Hon
          Yost and Natanis. If they waver,
          kill them.

Morgan leans on his long rifle and stares at the ground.

                    ARNOLD
          Yes?

                    MORGAN
          My fifty men here will fight in
          battle. On my turkey call they
          will climb trees. Fire upon
          British officers. In battle.
          They are not woods agents

A Screenplay

Arnold. Nor assassins.

              ARNOLD
General Arnold. You refuse an order?

              MORGAN
What you will.

Sullivan stops fiddling with the lamps and comes to Varick who lowers his manual and seems fascinated by the discussion.

              SULLIVAN
Lieutenant Varick, I must needs speak privately with you on an urgent matter.

              VARICK
It will wait, Sergeant.

Sullivan pulls on Varick's coat.

              SULLIVAN
Sir, it will not!

              ARNOLD
I could have you executed by firing squad.

              MORGAN
Shot you mean... if you must. If not, Washington has need of my services.

Varick looks back to hear as he reluctantly follows Sullivan away from the practice area.

Betrayal

                    VARICK
        What can be so powerfully
        urgent, Sullivan?

                    ARNOLD
        You don't think I'll do it, do
        you, Morgan!

                    MORGAN
        You have the stomach for it --
        if it suits your fancy.

Varick confronts Sullivan.

                    VARICK
        You need to know, Sergeant, that
        I will not be dragged about by -

                    SULLIVAN
        What needs knowing, Sir, is that
        I have witnessed this same scene
        with these two principal actors
        outside the walls of Quebec.
        They do not so much like each
        other, but they fight well in
        concert despite each having more
        pride than -

                    VARICK
        Is -- is there a point to be
        made?

                    SULLIVAN
        I fear Colonel Morgan will, in
        the hearing of others, say too
        much.

And General Arnold will feel obliged to
exert his authority. What we do not hear

may save Morgan's career and of consequence many American lives.

As Varick considers, Sullivan turns and calls toward Arnold's tent.

>SULLIVAN
>General Arnold, the gallows is almost ready and Chief Natanis seems anxious to be on his way.

>ARNOLD
>You're interrupt -- yes. Thank you, Sergeant Sullivan. His title is 'Sachem.'

As Arnold leaves Morgan, he calls back.

>ARNOLD
>Would asking for a few timely turkey calls offend your sharpshooters' sensibilities, Colonel Morgan?

His frown turns quickly to a broad smile.

>ARNOLD
>Where is my great and good friend Natanis, honored sachem of the proud Abnaki nation.

Natanis seems ready to smile or frown.

>NATANIS
>Mmmmmm.

>ARNOLD
>Natanis! Old friend!

Betrayal

NATANIS
How many Hunger Moons since The Dark Eagle pledged old friend Natanis 1,000 pounds?

ARNOLD
Even longer since our council The Congress paid The Dark Eagle's expenses. But I honor my debts for Quebec. You have my word. I shall pay if it takes me the rest of my life.

NATANIS
How long does The Dark Eagle plan to live? Do I have the Redcoats' pledge to aim low and not pierce his heart?

ARNOLD
They seem interested only in this leg. Despite your vision of The Dark Eagle soaring and falling, I shall live long enough to repay you in full. And I shall double the amount to 2,000 pounds.

NATANIS
The Great Arnold -- The Dreaded Dark Eagle -- has command of the winds. One thousand pounds unpaid is now blown into two thousand pounds -- unpaid.

ARNOLD
I will require from my friend a minor service for doubling the amount.

A Screenplay

                    NATANIS
          A minor service? Drive Burgoyne
          back to Canada. Swim The Great
          Lake and shoot Third Father
          George? Teach the birds to sing
          rebel songs? If The Dark Eagle
          is my friend, why do I tremble
          so.

                    ARNOLD
          A minor service, a small vision
          conveyed to the Mohawks at Fort
          Stanwix. We will relieve the
          fort with little bloodshed and a
          grateful Congress will repay me
          immediately. And I you.

                    NATANIS
          I will be able to reflect when
          my pouch is not so light as air.

Varick whispers to Sullivan.

                    VARICK
          That sounds suspiciously like
          extortion to me, Sergeant.

                    SULLIVAN
          By which party, Sir?

Arnold and Natanis move away side by
side, Arnold gesturing and talking
incessantly, Natanis reacting with
bemused frowns and few words.

On the drill field one of Morgan's men
finishes telling a humorous story.

Betrayal

Several smile.

Morgan guffaws, drawing a surprised look from Arnold who turns and then narrows his eyes.

							CUT TO:

(End of fourth hour)

EXT. DEEP WOODS - DUSK

Principal is rushing through the woods heedless of the scratches he is receiving from branches.

Second Runner tries to protect his face and catch up.

			SECOND RUNNER
	We can not leave her here.
	Do you wish the wolves to
	get her? That is the
	coward's way. She will haunt you
	forever.

			PRINCIPAL
	Leave her be. She is a child of
	the sun.

			SECOND RUNNER
	She is your enemy. She is a weak
	white woman. But she will live
	in your heart forever. She will
	poison your life with my
	sister. Our longhouse will be
	tainted.

A Screenplay

> PRINCIPAL
> She is innocent.

> SECOND RUNNER
> She is of her people. They come
> in white skins and red coats and
> blue coats and green coats. They
> come for your land and your
> water and your skin and bones.
> They light your funeral pyre...
> She has bewitched you.

Principal stops and shakes his head and then his entire body. He stops shaking and becomes erect and rigid.

Second Runner comes close and whispers. His hand is on his tomahawk.

> SECOND RUNNER
> I will cleanse you of her.

Principal shakes his head to indicate no.

He places his hand on Second Runner's chest to restrain him.

Principal moves away a few paces, stares at the sky, looks at the ground.

> CUT TO:

EXT. GREEN NEAR ARNOLD'S CAMP - DAY

Piggott is putting a platoon of militia through maneuvers as Varick watches.

Farther away Sullivan is watching as he listens to Arnold.

Betrayal

When Arnold leaves, Sullivan comes closer and sits on the ground.

After a few moves, Piggott calls a halt and begins instructing the platoon in the manual of arms.

Sullivan jumps to his feet and charges onto the field.

              SULLIVAN
    Corporal Piggott, I distinctly
    ordered flanking movements, did
    I not?

              PIGGOTT
    You may have, Sergeant Sullivan,
    but I felt the men needed more
    drill on the manual of arms.

              SULLIVAN
    I distinctly remember telling
    you not to feel nor think, did I
    not?

              PIGGOTT
    Would you like to feel my
    knuckles in your eye socket. I
    think you might not.

              SULLIVAN
    You bag of putrid wind! When I
    give an order you will obey it.

Sullivan puts his head down and runs toward Piggott.

              PIGGOTT
    If it makes sense to me, I might

A Screenplay

-- Uhhh!

Sullivan tackles Piggott and they roll on the ground. Their men break ranks and sit or smoke and chat or wander off.

A few sutler's wives take the opportunity to hawk foods and clothes.

No one except Varick pays attention to the wildly swinging, grunting, whirling mass that is a combination of Sullivan and Piggott's arms and legs in motion.

> VARICK
> This is disgraceful! Get up! Stop!

Sullivan and Piggott continue wrestling and swinging wildly.

> VARICK
> Have you no shame? You are to set examples for the men! Where is your pride!

As Piggott is biting Sullivan's leg, Sullivan is punching him in the ear.

> VARICK
> This is treason!

Sullivan releases his hold on Piggott and sits up.

Betrayal

              SULLIVAN
  How can this be treasonable,
  Sir?
Piggott takes advantage of the break to rise to his knees and aim a short punch to Sullivan's eye.

Sullivan grabs his eye and holds up his hand to signal Piggott to stop which he does immediately.

              VARICK
  You are giving comfort to the
  enemy! If they learn that there
  is dissesion in our ranks—

              SULLIVAN
  Dissension! Corporal Piggott and
  I are exchanging views on
  training emphasis. No dissension
  here. Corporal?

              PIGGOTT
  None whatsomeever, Sergeant
  Sullivan. I could get something
  for that eye.

              SULLIVAN
  Thank you kindly. Dandelion wine
  might help. And, Good Corporal,
  Our General wants to spread
  some unhappiness among the
  Mohawks. I would take it kindly
  if you should choose to
  recruit twenty hard men at Fort
  Stanwix for dark duty and
  personally lead said force.

A Screenplay

> PIGGOTT
> It would be my distinctive
> pleasure, Sergeant.

Varick watches as Sullivan and Piggott go off together chatting, gesturing, starting to argue again.

They raise their voices, look back quickly to see where Varick is, drop their voices and resume walking and talking quietly but intensely.

FADE OUT

EXT. CLEARING AT TOP OF HILL - NIGHT (HAZY MOON)

Jane is fashioning a bed of grasses and ferns and unrolling her blanket.

She hears something and looks up. Footsteps are heard.

CONTINUED:

Principal steps from the forest, a tear in his eye.

> JANE
> Ohh. Principal. I'm so glad to
> see you. I was getting
> worried. You and Second
> Runner have been gone so -- what
> is the matter?... You look so
> sad... Principal?

Principal offers Jane a bunch of dandelions as he looks at the moon.

She smiles and leans forward to take and smell the flowers. Principal takes his knife from its sheath.

                                          CUT TO:

EXT. BURGOYNE'S CAMP - DAY

Burgoyne is directing his mistress in a scene from Sheridan's <u>A School for Scandal</u>.

Clusters of soldiers and their women observe and whisper. A few Mohawks at first seem puzzled.

They laugh and shove each other whenever Burgoyne's mistress giggles.

Sergeant Burbank rides into camp with Chief Joseph Brant who turns off toard the Mohawk encampment.

                    BURGOYNE
        It's the daily argument about expenses. Sir Peter Teazle sermonizes. Lady Teazle argues that her expenditures are necessary to keep her in the fashion of the day. Sir Peter: 'The fashion indeed! What had you to do with the fashion when you married me?' Now you, My Dear. Lady Teazle is flippant, tossing off her lines, deliberately driving Sir Peter into a snit. This is Sheridan, My Sweet, light and frothy, the rage of London this spring.

A Screenplay

              MISTRESS
'For my part, I should think you would like to have your wife thought a –

She giggles softly. Burgoyne shakes his head.

              MISTRESS
-- a woman of taste.'

              BURGOYNE
We can do without your little giggles, My Dear. As actors, our discipline allows the audience to enjoy the play. Sir Peter: 'Aye -- there again -- taste. Zounds! Madam, you had no taste when you married me.'

Burgoyne's Mistress smiles broadly.

She tries throughout to suppress her giggling.

              MISTRESS
'That's very true -- (giggles) -- indeed -- (giggles) Sir Peter (sniffs, holds in giggle) and after having married you, I am sure I should never -- (giggling for several seconds while trying to stifle it; shouts end of line) -- pretend to taste again!

She breaks into uncontrollable giggling and laughing. Burgoyne starts to admonish her.

Betrayal

He slips into laughter.
Sergeant Burbank tries to get Burgoyne's attention.

SERGEANT BURBANK Your Excellency?

                  MISTRESS
   Oh Johnny, Johnny, it's so funny —

She giggles and laughs and whoops.

              SERGEANT BURBANK
   General Burgoyne, a most urgent
   matter.

Burgoyne frowns at Burbank.

Burgoyne looks back at his mistress who is trying in vain to control herself.

                  BURGOYNE
   Madam, how ever shall I prepare
   you for the Albany stage, never
   mind New York or London, if you
   insist on enjoying yourself.

                  MISTRESS
   I'll be good, Johnny. Promise.

She clears her throat

                  MISTRESS
   Ahem. 'But now, Sir Peter, since
   we have finished our daily
   jangle, I presume I may go to my
   engagement at Lady Sneerwell's.'
   It's soon funny, Johnny. How,
   she asks, can she possibly

pretend to taste having married
this booby.

               BURGOYNE
     That last line was exquisite.
     Now, Sir Peter: 'Aye, there's
     another precious circumstance --
     a charming set of acquaintance
     you have made -- '

            SERGEANT BURBANK
     (O.S.) Begging Your Excellency's
     pardon, a murder most bloody.

               BURGOYNE
     Murder?

He glances at his mistress.

She has not heard; is still trying to
suppress chuckles and giggles.

               BURGOYNE
     Excuse me, Dearest, I'll be but
     a minute.

Burgoyne descends a few stairs of the
stage. He looks archly at Sergeant Burbank.

Phillips hurries in, steps behind Burbank,
and signals him to continue.

               BURGOYNE
     Have you no sensibility,
     Sergeant! There is a lady
     present.

            SERGEANT BURBANK
     A lady has been cruelly

murdered, General Burgoyne, by one of the savages. A minister's daughter from the Mohawk valley.

          PHILLIPS
Come to join our new Captain Timmons -his fiancee, Miss McCrae.

          BURGOYNE
Find the Indian -- not the savage, Sergeant -- and hang him. Send out a patrol for any accomplices. Phillips, you may inform our captain. Is that all?

          SERGEANT BURBANK
He is here, Sir, the Mohawk captain Principal, with Miss Jane McCrea's bloody scalp in his belt. Chief Joseph Brandt has just ridden in my company from Fort Stanwix to demand his release.

          PHILLIPS
On one of His Majesty's horses. Brandt says the tribe will punish him or not when the campaign is over.

          BURGOYNE
Punish him -- or not! That will never do. Hang the savage -- the Indian -- and have done with it!

          PHILLIPS
Chief Joseph Brandt is needed at

A Screenplay

Fort Stanwix. The Mohawks are in a dangerous state. But he will not return there until you have released Principal.

BURGOYNE
I'll pardon him -- once we have stretched his neck.

PHILLIPS
We will lose all our Indian allies if we hang him. They already feel that you -that we have tricked them into killing their brothers, the Oneida, at Oriskany Creek. Barry St. Leger fears that their murderous mood will spare no settlers, rebel or Tory -- on their march home. There will be fire and blood along the Mohawk.

SERGEANT BURBANK
if we do not hang -- the murderer -- all those leaning to the King will turn away -- protect their own -- join the reb -

PHILLIPS
Sergeant, you are free to resume your duties at Fort Stanwix.

Burbank heads for his horse slowly, hoping to catch another word or two.

Burgoyne rubs his temples.

Betrayal

PHILLIPS
Please, Sir. If St. Leger is to join you at Albany he needs all of his Mohawks.

BURGOYNE
All right, all right, I wash my hands of the whole affair. Tell Brandt he may have his precious murderer. May I resume now, if it please you?

PHILLIPS
Chief Brandt is waiting for you at his tent. He has drawn up an official document remanding Principal to Six Nations' justice.

BURGOYNE
I am to wait on him! I am to do his bidding? Are you mad, Phillips? He can grow old waiting for me to wait on him. And... take back the King's horse.

PHILLIPS
This may be a time to bend, John, if our mission is to succeed.

BURGOYNE
The Mohawks are in a dangerous state. Our loyal settlers will bleed into the Mohawk. And I must bend to an educated savage. You would do well on the stage, William -- in melodrama. Do they

A Screenplay

    bend? Do they compromise! What -
    - what are they doing?

Phillips and Burgoyne watch as several Mohawk braves lift Brandt's tent and move it half the distance to Burgoyne.

EXT. TREE STUMP IN FRONT OF BRANDT'S TENT - DAY

Burgoyne is bending over, signing a document.

He straightens up and hands the pen to Chief Joseph Brandt.

Colonel Phillips and a squad of redcoats leave Principal with his people as soon as Burgoyne signs. They all go off.

              BURGOYNE
    Chief Joseph, meaning no
    disrespect, what might be the
    fate of a murderer in your
    nations?

             CHIEF JOSEPH
    The only man who saw this deed
    is said to be gone to Canada.
    If a man is charged by
    another who saw the deed, he
    would be ostracized, shunned by
    all in his village, treated
    worse than a slave until the
    Great Council meets. If the dead
    woman were of our nation, her
    relatives would decide the
    punishment, usually death, or,
    for the vengeful, banishment

from our nations.

          BURGOYNE
That is a dreadful prospect,
Chief Brandt.

Brandt pauses to stare at Burgoyne before answering quietly.

          CHIEF JOSEPH
Not for someone like you who can afford to lose and gain friends weekly in the great dark city of London. Life in our longhouses is not so fickle. We learn within our place in the sun to live with each other. Banishment therefore is worse than death for most of us.

          BURGOYNE
Of course it is.

          CHIEF JOSEPH
I must return to my men now at Fort Stanwix. They have spilled the blood of their brothers the Oneida. They look in vain for the easy journey promised by the great Burgoyne.

          BURGOYNE
Yesss... well... fortunes of war. No guarantees. Do please convey my compliments to Barry -
- General St. Leger that is.

          CHIEF JOSEPH
I shall. To both.

A Screenplay

Burgoyne raises an eyebrow as he watches Brandt move quickly off.

> BURGOYNE
> Sharp mind... for a savage. Have a pleasant stroll.

Burgoyne turns and calls to his mistress who has left the stage.

> BURGOYNE
> Act Two, My Darling. Sans giggles.
> Oh... gone early for our nap.
> Phillips? Where has –

He is alone.

FADE OUT EXT. HILL EN ROUTE TO FORT STANWIX – DAY

A Tory DISPATCH RIDER in a green jacket stops at a well and draws water in his hat for his horse and himself.

His horse is nervous.

The rider looks up and sees another dispatch rider swinging from a tree.

He starts, then reads the sign pinned to the body:

> INSERT which READS:
> "Mad George's friend -- Death to all Tories!"

The rider throws the remaining water over his head and leaps onto his horse.

Betrayal

As he gallops off a shot rings out.
He is shot in the arm, straightens up and drops the reins.

He grabs the reins with his good hand, hugs and spurs his horse.

CUT TO:

EXT. BURGOYNE'S CAMP - DAY

Burgoyne and his mistress are drinking from champagne glasses.

They are nibbling at rich confections and exchanging humorous remarks.

He takes a proclamation from a worried-looking Phillips and scans it.

Burgoyne's mistress frolics in the background with a small dog wearing a royal crest on its woolen jacket.

>MISTRESS
>Will he be too warm, Johnny, or will the evening be coolish?

>PHILLIPS
>Your Excellency, we must inform Captain Timmons of his fiancee's fate. All day he has been asking after her and Hon Yost and his Indian friends.

>BURGOYNE
>We will hear his reaction to the proclamation first. Elsewise he

A Screenplay

would be of little use to us.
A corporal escorts Burt who is dressed in his red captain's uniform to them.

Burt clicks to attention and salutes smartly.

He attempts to speak softly to Phillips who pretends not to hear and speaks in a loud voice.

                BURT
Is there any news of Ja –

              PHILLIPS
General Burgoyne wishes you to hear a passage from the proclamation you will be carrying to your neighbors in the Mohawk Valley. It will be issued throughout the colony of New York and further.

              BURGOYNE
Yes. This passage I wished you to hear, Captain Timmons. I have offered the olive branch to all families hereabouts—loyal, rebel, doubtful twixt here and Fort Stanwix and Albany if they instantly swear fealty to the King and support my army wholeheartedly. Should they foolishly resist however, I have this remedy for their defection. Colonel Phillips, if you please.

Phillips raises the proclamation to arm's

length and reads in stentorian tones.
              PHILLIPS
    'To remedy misconduct or
    disloyalty to the King and his
    emissaries, I have but to give
    stretch to my Indian friends
    and I have thousands at hand' –

              BURGOYNE
    Etcetera, etcetera -- how will
    your neighbors react to that
    discipline, Young Captain from
    the Mohawk Valley?

Burt is astonished. He has trouble speaking. Burgoyne smiles encouragement.

              BURT
    They will ki -- kill you, Sir,
    with mus -- muskets or with
    neglect.

Finally reached to his core, Burgoyne starts.

              BURGOYNE
    What! What did you say, Young
    Man!

              BURT
    The leaners on the middle of the
    fence will jump now to the
    Rebels to ss -- save themselves
    from the sssavages. Everyone
    will hide their foodstuffs in
    the earth and drive their
    cattle into the deep woods.
    Your army will have twigs and
    insects to eat should you iss –

- issue this ma -- as -- aad proclamation.

BURGOYNE
This WHAT!!!

PHILLIPS
Sir, he did not mean -- he speaks plain and direct -

BURGOYNE
I want him GONE! Out of my camp, Phillips. He is a rebel disguised as a Loyalist.

PHILLIPS
I will send him to the valley with the proclamations. But we must speak to him about -

BURGOYNE
If he is not gone this instant, his life shall pay the forfeit. No one talks to me in such a manner. No one!

PHILLIPS
No, Sir. No one does.

EXT. FORT STANWIX - NIGHT SERIES OF SHOTS

Piggott leads a small raiding party out of Fort Stanwix's sally port to the Mohawk encampment.

A fire is set in the last row of tents which attracts all of the Mohawks.

A Redcoat and a Tory who remain at their

posts between the Mohawk and British and Tory encampments are knocked unconscious by the raiders.

The raiders shred the English suits and take all the valuables they can carry.

Piggott and a few raiders slip into the British encampment and hide hats and pieces of suits in the tents.

EXT. OUTSKIRTS OF BURGOYNE'S CAMP - DUSK
Burt stands by his horse.

Phillips hands him copies of Burgoyne's proclamation. salutes, and leaves.

Burt tries to pack them in his saddlebag but fumbles. Arthur packs the proclamations and helps him mount.

                    ARTHUR
    Better now, Friend. They ask hard
    questions and want soft answers.

Burt rides through the crowded lanes of the camp with his head down. He hardly sees the legs of soldiers and their women playing cards, drinking, ducking into tents, bargaining.

Burt slows to stare at a blonde scalp hanging from a warrior's belt.

He looks up and recognizes Principal whose face is scratched. He reins his horse.

Principal flinches and then slips away through the noisy crowd.

A Screenplay

Burt turns his horse about violently.

>   BURT
>   Sss -- stop him! Colonel Phillips!
>   Principal! Arthur!

Burt wheels his horse in a circle but can make no headway. DISSOLVE TO:

SERIES OF SHOTS

A) Burt on horseback is meandering through the forest with Arthur following him on foot at a distance

B) Burt is sitting on the ground as Arthur builds a fire using some of the proclamations as starter

C) Burt is holding a cup of tea staring into space as Arthur feeds him. Burt's uniform coat is on the ground, the right sleeve beginning to burn.

D) Piggott quietly approaches through the trees.

E) Piggott watches Paulus and two of his cohorts creep up on Burt and Arthur.

F) Piggott moves behind them and draws his hunting knife.

>   MOVE TO:

EXT. ARNOLD'S CAMP - DAY

Burt is led up the stairs of the gallows.

Betrayal

Arthur fights back tears as he watches. Paulus and his two cohorts wait to be paid for capturing Burt.

Varick comes out of his tent holding a letter to see Hon Yost dancing and playing his Jew's harp in the shadow of the gallows.

Varick stops beside Arnold and opens the letter.

INSERT: We HEAR Jane's voice as Varick READS:

> JANE
> (V.O.) Dear Richard, Forgive me. I do not detest you. I shall always love you. But now like a brother. Thank you for all the arguments and your passionate love. You know me as your Jenny, a fractious female, yet love me still. Burton places a tremendous burden on me by agreeing with everything I say. Perhaps his stammering ways hold back his real opinions. But he did not stammer, he did not hesitate when he told me, 'I love you Jane McCrae and will not live without you.' It terrified me but I would not have him change one word. I go to join Burton with Burgoyne. Love Always, Your Jenny/Burton's Jane.

Varick looks up at the gallows dully.

A Screenplay

Varick does not realize that it is Burt until the hangman starts to tie a blindfold.

              VARICK
  Burt? By God, it is Burt.

              ARNOLD
  What? Do you know the man?

Varick SEES Flashes of:

Jane in the belfry, juggling, dancing into the kitchen, passing in the company of Principal, pulling Burt down to kiss him goodbye, her signature: "Your Jenny/Burton's Jane"

              ARNOLD
  Lieutenant Varick! Do you know
  this man! Is he enemy!

              VARICK
  He is a Tory... he is my half-
  brother.

              ARNOLD
  Your brother!

Arnold is truly shocked.

He stares at Varick a split second, then turns to shout in the direction of the gallows.

              ARNOLD
  Stop! Bring that man to me! Are
  you mad, Varick? Because he is
  Tory, you would have your own

Betrayal

brother swing without word one.

Arnold turns back to see Varick racing to Burt.

As soon as his hands are untied, Burt reaches to spring the trap and hang himself.

Burt jumps through the open trap door. He claws at the rope around his neck.

              VARICK
  NOOOOOOOO!

He arrives just in time to catch Burt.

Varick staggers but does not fall as Burt's head is jerked to the left.

              BURT
  Let me go.

             ARNOLD
  There is no cause, no principle
  that supercedes loyalty to one's
  family.

              PAULUS
  I still get my capture money?
  I'm entitled!

              ARNOLD
  If that -- Paulus -- opens his
  mouth again, hang him. Where is
  Hon Yost?

Hon Yost is pushed out, his Jew's harp in his mouth, his hands tied behind his back.

A Screenplay

He is trying to smile and play a tune simultaneously.

The shy private uses his musket stock to gently prod Yost forward.

He drops his Jew's harp and gets down on his knees, pushing his face in the dirt to get it back in his mouth.

Varick gently lowers Burt to the ground.

Piggott draws his knife and twirls it to warn Paulus away from Arnold.

Mrs. Yost rushes to help Hon Yost to his feet and unties him as she speaks to Arnold.

              MRS. YOST
He's a sweet simple boy, General. He means no harm... he thinks it a game.

              VARICK
Burt? Oh God Burt, I'm sorry. I -- I was -- thinking.

              BURT
Slit my throat, Richard. Ease me over.

              ARNOLD
The game is over for him, Missus Yost. The only saving act/grace now would be for him to deliver a message to the enemy force at Stanwix.

Betrayal

               VARICK
Stop it, Burt. You're all right
now.

               BURT
All right? She is dead Richard.
What is all right.

               VARICK
Who? Mother McCrae? who's dead?

               BURT
Jane. Killed and scalped by
Principal her scalp on
Principal's belt.

               VARICK
No -- I have her letter here.
Sullivan and I saw her in the
woods but a few days... No...
she can't be.

               BURT
Puh -- paraded around Burgoyne's
camp.

               VARICK
NOOO!

               ARNOLD
Lieutenant Varick! I need you!

Varick turns in a daze toward Arnold's
voice.

               MRS. YOST
He'll do whatever you say,
General. Won't you Hon?

A Screenplay

Hon Yost smiles.

He props his jacket on two sticks so the main part is protected by a tree trunk and invites Daniel Morgan's men to fire at the sleeves.

                      CUT TO:

EXT. BRITISH SIEGE OUTSIDE FORT STANWIX - MORNING

On hills near the camps of Mohawk, Tory, and British forces which are laying siege to Fort Stanwix, many Mohawks are tending to elevated funeral pyres with smoke filling the sky.

On the lowest hill Natanis prays and feeds into his circular fire bits of London suits and hats left from the rebel raid on the Mohawk encampment.

He is surrounded by a few skeptical Tories and dozens of attentive Mohawk warriors. Many are bruised and bandaged from the fighting at Oriskany Creek...

Nearby some are packing their baggage and preparing to leave

                NATANIS
     I have seen The Dark Eagle
     soaring above... turkeys
     singing in trees... rivers of
     blood washing the captains of
     The Six Nations to The Great
     lake.. red warriors and white
     Tories... The Dark Eagle...

Betrayal

       blocking out the sun.

Hon Yost runs past into the British camp.

Mohawk and Tory pickets move toward him.
He is caught and held from falling in
front of St. Leger's tent.

                    HON YOST
          Dark Eagle.

St. Leger rushes from his tent without his
coat to push the noisy, nervous Mohawks
and whispering, intense Tories aside and
command Hon Yost's attention.

                    ST.LEGER
          Arnold? How close? How many
          troops?

                    HON YOST
          (gasping) On -- my heels.

                    ST.LEGER
          How many soldiers -- Washington
          could not release troops unless
          -- where is Sir William Howe --
          he would not sail south -- how
          many you fool?

St. Leger and the Mohawks and Tories and
a few Redcoats who have come from the
siege ditches watch Hon Yost closely as
he looks down, around, then up and
extends his arm to indicate that Arnold
has as many troops as there are leaves on
the trees--thousands.

A Screenplay

> ST. LEGER
> He cannot! Who paid you to spread these lies. If he raised more than a thousand they would all be farmers who run at the first peal of cannon thunder.

Several Mohawks wounded at Oriskany Creek murmur 'farmers.' or 'Dark Eagle.'

St. Leger's voice rises and becomes more strident as the noise and uneasiness mounts.

> ST. LEGER
> Militia! Look at me, you fool! Are they all raw militia?

Still catching his breath, Hon Yost takes his jacket half off and holds up his arm to let his bullet-creased sleeve dangle.

> HON YOST
> Dan'l Morgan... long rifles.

> ST. LEGER
> Arrest that man! If he resists, shoot him. I will not have traitors in my camp. Washington would not release Morgan's sharpshooters unless Howe... The fool lies -- he has been paid -- we will hang him as an example to all who spread -

At first Tories and Redcoats whisper 'Arnold.'

The Mohawks and Tories and Redcoats all

repeat Morgan's and Arnold's names louder
and talk excitedly.

Some Mohawks circle protectively around Hon
Yost. Natanis steps forward to address St.
Leger.

> NATANIS
> I have seen Redcoats wearing
> King hats and rivers of blood -

> ST.LEGER
> We do not require your mad
> mumblings. Where is Chief Joseph
> Brandt?

> SERGEANT BURBANK
> He is not back yet from
> Skenesborough in the Jenny
> McRae affair.

Indians, Tories, and Redcoats make way
for the TORY DISPATCH RIDER.

The Young Private speaks quietly but
urgently to Sergeant Burbank

> PRIVATE
> Can't we beat him back? Why are
> the savages so disturbed by
> Arnold?

> SERGEANT BURBANK
> They know. He'll come on
> now. Hell or high water. Bring
> fire and shot and death with
> him. We keep drubbing Arnold and
> he keeps coming on. And if he
> has Daniel Morgan's rifles with

him you'll hear turkey calls.
Don't stand next an
officer. They are all
dead of an afternoon.

The Mohawks back away murmuring and start
through the British encampment.

One tomahawks a British tent.

Another emerges from a tent with a jug of
rum.

A third rummages nearby in the young
private's tent.

The bloodied Tory dispatch rider dismounts
and stumbles toward St. Leger.

>   ST.LEGER
> Sergeant Burbank, take a squad
> and drive those savages away
> from our encampment.

>   SERGEANT BURBANK
> More like a regiment might do.
> First squad here! Clubbed
> muskets!

>   TORY RIDER
> General St. Leger? Sir William
> Howe has sailed for Chesapeake
> Bay. Intent on capturing
> Congress in Philadelphia. He
> will not be joining you at
> Albany.

Betrayal

          ST.LEGER
When! He must support us! Call him back! Burgoyne must call—

          TORY RIDER
A week or more he sailed from the City of New York. I am the third rider dispatched. I found the second swinging from a tree and just escaped the rebel rangers. There will be no juncture of the great armies, Sir. It is you and Gentleman John -- General Burgoyne -now.

A Mohawk warrior holds up a London hat which he has found in the young private's tent.

          MOHAWK
King hat!

          ST.LEGER
Bring the cannon about! Get the regulars from the ditches!

A turkey call sounds.

An aide runs up with St. Leger's bright red uniform coat which he tuns inside out to wear the dun-colored lining on the outside.

The young private backs away from St. Leger and into the Mohawk who is furiously ransacking the private's tent.

          PRIVATE
I didn't touch your bloody

A Screenplay

>   precious suit and I won't stand
>   your turning my tent out, you
>   greasy savage.

The Mohawk stuns the young private with a tomahawk blow. A series of turkey calls sound from different directions.

EXT. BRITISH, TORY, AND MOHAWK CAMPS - NOON
SERIES OF SHOTS of Hon Yost

A)   Playing with remains of derby hat as British squad tries vainly to drive the Mohawks away from the tents and supplies and baggage

B)   Climbing a tree and making a loud turkey call and smiling as nearby veteran British officers flinch

C)   Smearing his face with ashes as chaos reigns in Indian and British and Tory camps. The Mohawks pause only long enough to cut down and scalp a few white allies.

D)   Walking to the front gate of Fort Stanwix alone and knocking on the sally port until a rebel militia man opens the small door cautiously to peer out.

>   HON YOST
>   All gone.

                                    MOVE TO:

INT.   FORT STANWIX - NIGHT

A wild celebration is in full sway.

Betrayal

An impromptu band with Sergeant Sullivan beating spoons on a kettle is playing and singing "The World Turned Upside Down."

Daniel Morgan and Piggott are dancing as wildly as Hon Yost and the drunken militia men who held the fort.

Arnold is dancing stiffly by himself. Varick studies the scene for a moment.

As soon as he sees Varick, Arnold stops dancing and quickly approaches

>ARNOLD
>I have no compunction in releasing your half-brother to your custody, but others will question it. Why didn't Arnold hang him? A British officer out of uniform with damning papers. Let them cavil. I care not a fig for any of them. In return, however, Lieutenant Varick, I expect that you will suppress your grief long enough to accompany Sergeant Sullivan on a recruiting trip for Saratoga troops.

Varick nods.

He hugs Burt who is hunched over on a mule with a blanket around him and leads him out the open front gate.

Franks leads Morgan's sharpshooters jibing and jeering into the fort double time where they disperse without waiting for orders.

Franks waves a salute to Varick.

> FRANKS
> He'll want you back to recruit for Saratoga.

Varick does not respond.

We HEAR "The World Turned Upside Down" sung or shouted by all.

FADE OUT EXT./INT. WILLIAM PITT TAVERN - NIGHT
Sullivan dismounts and waits.

Varick sits woodenly in the saddle after his horse stops.

> SULLIVAN
> How old was Miss McCrae?

Varick looks at Sullivan a moment before answering.

> VARICK
> She was twenty-two... almost twenty-three... ww -- why do you ask?

> SULLIVAN
> Too old by far -- practically an old maid.

Sullivan heads for the taproom. Varick dismounts quickly and follows. INT. WILLIAM PITT TAVERN - NIGHT The tavern is full.

Betrayal

Jonathan Paulus and his cronies are in their customary places leaning on the bar.

The drunken farmer has passed out at a table.

> PAULUS
> We risked our lives to capture that British spy but Arnold was slow to pay us our capture money.

> INNKEEPER
> Then you be quicker in paying some of your bill here.

Paulus searches for a reply until he spots Sullivan and Varick.

> PAULUS
> The young lieutenant come back to urge us stick our bellies in front of cold British steel. Leave our warm beds and wives and children to the mercy of savages while we sleep on wet ground. How much do they pay you to say these damnably foolish things to us?

Varick stands silently watching Sullivan.

Sullivan steps forward.

He makes a show of slapping money on the bar.

> SULLIVAN
> Come Boys, it's my turn to

stand the tariff for a bowl of punch. Innkeeper! Your largest bowls. Your best wine and rum. No stinting. No water. I must tell my friends here about the bloody horrible fate of the beautiful Jenny McCrae.

PAULUS
We heard something -- she was a minister's daughter?

SULLIVAN
Torn from her home by drunken savages, forced in the very fields -- rather than submit to—

VARICK
What in God's name are you saying? You know she was en route to—

SULLIVAN
Forgive Lieutenant Varick. He loved sixteen-year-old Jenny McCrae and had hoped that she -- but it was his Tory half-brother Burt who won her -

VARICK
Sullivan, I'll kill you. I'll carve you in little pieces and feed you to the pigs.

SULLIVAN
Be gentle with the young officer, Men. He is sore distraught. His mind is addled with grief.

Betrayal

>   VARICK
> You're dead, Sullivan! I will
> roast you alive.

>   SULLIVAN
> Perhaps you had best bind him
> and stop up that infernal
> mouth. I feel for him, but my
> ears are worn ragged.

Some men bind Varick.

Paulus takes a sweat-stained bandanna from his neck and sticks it in Varick's mouth.

More men gather around Sullivan or stare at Varick.

>   SULLIVAN
> But wait. Some may not have
> dined yet. I would not spoil
> your supper with this bloody
> tale.

Several urge Sullivan to continue.

The drunken farmer wakes up, tries to focus on what is happening, but nods off.

>   SULLIVAN
> She was a sweet young thing just
> ripening past girlhood. Like
> many, from a divided family.
> Brother Thomas a surgeon with
> Washington. Brother Joseph
> an officer with Sir William
> Howe in New York City. Her
> mother sympathized with us
> it was said, but her tormented

A Screenplay

> Presbyterian divine of a father guided her. Jenny McCrae had young ideas, soft, sweet questions: 'Isn't the King our protector?' Reverend McCrae's answers led her inevitably down the Tory path to perdition...

CLOSE-UP

Varick stops struggling with his bonds to remember the true Jane.

EXT. MCCRAE FARM - DAY

Varick is on horseback jiggling soil in his hand as he surveys the farm acreage.

Jane rides slightly behind him, then spurs her horse and tries to catch up. Varick rides away.

> JANE
> You're a fool, Richard! There is no reason to break with the King except greed. You are the tool, the pawn, the whipping boy of greedy, avaricious men. Fight and die so Arnold and Hancock can bribe port inspectors while we sweat the soil. So Washington and Jefferson can live in mansions and whip slaves to their work. How can you be so blind!

BACK TO SCENE

Varick stares a minute before realizing

that the tavern patrons are quiet as they gather closer to hear Sullivan who has paused.

> SULLIVAN
> Her lovely blonde locks on the belt of a savage. Treacherous savages sent by that British popinjay Gentleman Johnny Burgoyne. This is his promise.

Sullivan throws Burgoyne's proclamations on the table, startling the drunken farmer awake.

> PAULUS
> We read his proclamation to the Indians.

> INNKEEPER
> We laughed, God forgive us, at this proclamation threatening savage reprisals. We did not think him capable of—

> SULLIVAN
> I speak only for myself. Go home and look to your daughters. The image of mine is graven in my heart.

Sullivan pauses and raises his right hand. I pledge to join Gates's army and fight alongside Arnold and Morgan until the savages and Tories and Bloody John Burgoyne are driven from this land. If any are ready now, we have papers to sign. Three months and we will have rid

A Screenplay

          DRUNKEN FARMER
  I'll sign now! The bastards!

The drunken farmer bangs into a table and falls in his haste to reach Sullivan.

Varick is startled as thirty men eagerly push into a semblance of a line to join up.

Sullivan unties Varick.

DISSOLVE TO: SERIES OF SHOTS

A) Varick and Sullivan riding and arguing

B) Sullivan speaking in another tavern and Varick signing up men.

C) Sullivan telling a story as they ride and Varick laughing softly, reluctantly, and shaking his head

D) Sullivan yielding the floor to Varick

          VARICK
  She was a sweet young girl
  unschooled in the ways of the
  world...

EXT. MOHAWK VALLEY WOODS - DAY Sullivan is tightening his saddle. Varick stares at him.

          SULLIVAN
  I ride to join Arnold in
  Philadelphia. Congress is ready
  to flee before Sir William Howe
  arrives, but they will court
  martial Our Little General

somewhere. Will you speak to
his indiscretions?

                VARICK
How can you care so much for
independence and care so little
about Arnold? He -

Sullivan mounts and leans toward Varick.

              SULLIVAN
It is the matter that matters
and not the man. The country,
not the citizen. Will you
testify before Congress what you
know about his dealings and
doings?

Varick turns away and looks down.

                VARICK
I don't think so. I don't
really care to. I have
fulfilled my duty to
recruit militia. I have no
interest in the politics of
war. My brother -

              SULLIVAN
How pure. How saintly. Remember
Richard Varick -- I did not ask
you to lie... but he may.

                VARICK
You are confusing my words.

              SULLIVAN
I can not clarify them. And you
can not sit on the fence this

whole war.

               VARICK
On the fence! I fight for my beliefs.

              SULLIVAN
If you have learned nothing from serving with Benedict Arnold, surely you see that conduct in the field is not enough... I wish you well, Richard Varick. You have done more than most. You –

Sullivan mounts and rides off.

Varick waves feebly.

Sullivan without turning around gives the thumbs-up sign and drops a money pouch on the ground as he spurs his horse.

               VARICK
You've left something behind. Sullivan!

FADE TO:

(End of hour Five)

EXT. AN INN NEAR PHILADELPHIA – EVENING

Arnold helps Peggy, who is dressed in a fashionable low-cut black mourning gown with a chest veil, into an ornate white coach with a fancy crest on the side door.

Sullivan rubs one of the four white

Betrayal

horses and watches Peggy. In the background liveried coachmen are entering the inn.

> ARNOLD
> The death of Miss Shippen's cousin Arthur has plunged her into grief, Sergeant. You'll find your way back to our lodgings while I endeavor to console her. When the coachmen finish their dinner I will carry her home.

> SULLIVAN
> If you mean, General, the lodgings that lie somewhere seven miles that way, I should find them. Eventually. If I am not first mistaken by cutthroats for an odd piece of baggage whose passion is stumbling about in the dark.

Arnold has not listened to a word. He climbs into the carriage.

> ARNOLD
> Yes. Coming Miss Shippen.

Sullivan sets off briskly.

He hums and then sings Yankee Doodle Dandy.

> SULLIVAN
> Father and I went down to camp A riding on a pony, stuck a feather in his cap And called it macaroni. Yankee Doodle keep it

up, Yankee Doodle Dandy! Dum de
dum dah diddy dum, And with the
girls be handy!

Sullivan glances back at the carriage which
is rocking gently.

He sees an angry mob of a dozen plainly-
dressed Levelers approach the carriage
door.

VICTOR KANE steps forward and tries to
pull open the locked door.

>	VICTOR KANE
> Come out you Tory bastard and
> bring the bitch with!

Sullivan turns and runs back
shouting.

> SULLIVAN
> You fools! That's General
> Arnold! Benedict Arnold!

Arnold springs from the carriage and
draws his sword. Two men down him with a
board and an axe handle.

Arnold cuts a third man as he falls, hits
his elbow, and drops his sword.

> VICTOR KANE
> I served with Arnold at Danbury.
> He'd never ride in a royalty
> coach with a Tory whore.

Sullivan picks up Arnold's sword and swings
wildly. Arnold pushes up on one arm and

draws a tiny pistol. He aims at the leader but does not fire.

> ARNOLD
> Kane?

> VICTOR KANE
> General?

> ARNOLD
> Victor Kane.

Arnold lowers his pistol.

He stands and breathes deeply before speaking.

Peggy moves to the coach's window. She reattaches her chest veil which was hanging to one side.

> ARNOLD
> Mister Kane I should like to present you to Miss Margaret Shippen, my fiancee, who is in mourning for her cousin Arthur, a captain fighting with General Washington in New Jersey. Miss Shippen, this is Mister Victor Kane who fought by my side when we warmly welcomed the British to Connecticut.

Kane gives a strained smile and almost bows but catches himself.

> ARNOLD
> Mister Kane wishes to apologize to you -while he still draws

breath.
Kane pulls his hat off.

          VICTOR KANE
  Oh yes! Yes Miss Shippen. I am
  grievous sorry. Please accept my
  humblest apologies. So say we
  all.
Kane waves his arm to include
his men who obviously do not
share his need to apologize.

They grumble and slink away despite his glare.

Kane catches the wounded Leveler who reluctantly turns back and removes his hat on Kane's urging.

Peggy smiles benevolently. Arnold watches.

He speaks to Sullivan in a low, intense voice as Peggy climbs down from the coach..

          ARNOLD
  Miss Shippen's father, Edward
  Shippen, is one of the finest
  gentleman I have ever met. To
  think that these Levelers --
  miserable scum -- Reed's
  henchmen -- are spying on him
  and his family. Rather than lift
  themselves up they want to drag
  everyone down to their low
  level. And my Peggy.

          SULLIVAN
  Fiancee?

Betrayal

>   ARNOLD
>   Practically. Her father
>   hesitates because of the age
>   difference. But this campaign
>   I am sure of.

Peggy moves to his side, places her hand on his forearm, and speaks softly.

>   PEGGY
>   This may be presumptuous of me,
>   General Arnold -

Arnold shakes his head vigorously to indicate that Peggy could say nothing presumptuous.

Before he can speak Peggy continues.

>   PEGGY
>   -- but I fear that this rabble
>   know not how to treat a man of
>   your quality. You will have to
>   look elsewhere for the
>   recognition you merit so fully.

Peggy sniffs and dabs at his forehead with a tiny lace handkerchief.

>   ARNOLD
>   Ah, Miss Shippen, don't shed a
>   tear on it. I have survived far
>   worse execrations.

Peggy and Arnold climb into the carriage. They move back, away from the window.

In the background Kane speaks quietly to his men.

A Screenplay

                SULLIVAN
   I'll be fine General.

There is no response from the carriage.

                SULLIVAN
   If we stay here much longer, we'll have to either dine on Sir William Howe's prison ship or Congress will send an armed guard to arrest us. I'll rub through and meet you early for our trip to York tomorrow.

Sullivan starts off. He calls back.

                SULLIVAN
   Try not to worry.

The carriage rocks gently.

Kane and a few of his men move toward Sullivan.

Sullivan stops humming and readies himself for a continuation of the scuffle.

                VICTOR KANE
   There may be desperate men in your path. Good men with worthless money taken to highway robbery. We will walk you a ways if you like.

Sullivan extends his hand to shake Kane's.

First Kane and then his men join Sullivan in humming and singing Yankee Doodle Dandy as they stride into the darkness.

              SULLIVAN
And there was Captain Washington, with grand folks all about him, They say he's grown so tarnal proud, He cannot ride without em.

              VICTOR KANE
Yankee Doodle keep it up, Yankee Doodle Dandy!

              ALL
Mind the music and the step, And with the girls be handy!

DISSOLVE TO: EXT. MCCRAE FARM - DAY

Burt sits outside the farmhouse, covered with blankets on a cloudy, windy day, staring rigidly into space.

Arthur sits quietly off to the side watching Burt.

In the backround Mrs. McCrae finishes reading from the Bible to Reverend McRae and rises.
Varick walks toward the maple tree, kicking and throwing pebbles down the road, looking every which way.

              MRS. MCCREA
Richard, she won't be meeting you here.

              VARICK
If Jenny were here, would

everything seem so gray -- all
color has drained -- I am sure I
loved this once, but it holds no
vibrancy for me now. But I will
overcome that I will make it
my business to farm -

          MRS. MCCREA
You have been merely a visitor
in the Valley, Richard, since
you came back from your year at
college. It seems your business
is elsewhere.

Varick and Mrs. McCrae turn to see a rider approaching.

          MRS. MCCREA
This may be it riding in now.
She loved you Richard -- even if
she knew she couldn't live with
you. We all love you. Go with
God -- if you can.

Franks trots in, dismounts, and dusts himself off.

          VARICK
Major Franks! How is The
General?

          FRANKS
How should he be.

Franks hands a letter to Varick.

Burt stands up to tend Franks' horse. He reaches for the reins, becomes dizzy, and stumbles.

Betrayal

Franks steadies Burt.

INSERT
We HEAR Arnold's voice as Varick READS:

           ARNOLD
(V.O.) Lieutenant Varick, I urgently require your assistance in York, Pennsylvania. Congress hides there. Nefarious men are lying through their teeth to destroy my reputation. I well remember that your generous testimony led to Phillip Schuyler's acquittal with honor. Not your fault that Granny Gates stole his place in The Northern Army. My career, my honor, my family name is at stake. Come to York. Justice requires your presence! Your devoted servant, General Benedict Arnold.

           VARICK
I can't come. I'm -- I'm needed here. I have not been paid -- I have no money -- of my own -

           FRANKS
I bring some earnest money for your travel.

           VARICK
I don't wish to engage in -- he lied to me about Burgoyne paying for scalps. He lied to Congress about Valcour receipts. He must know Smith is -

A Screenplay

> FRANKS
> Does he disappoint you, Richard Varick? Find another time to cry. He is our one best hope to stop Burgoyne.

Franks salutes Burt and mounts.

> FRANKS
> Being a liar and a thief does not preclude shrewdness and bravery in the field.

> VARICK
> You don't really like him!

> FRANKS
> It is not required.

Franks throws a heavy bag of coins to Varick and turns away.

> VARICK
> There is too much here. I don't need half this. And if I don't come?

> FRANKS
> It looks enough to carry you across the ocean. It has to have been personally done by –

> VARICK
> Counted out by General –

They both say "Arnold" at the same time and smile. Franks tips his hat and rides away.

Betrayal

INT. MILLINER'S SHOP - MORNING

Varick enters the milliner's shop and looks at a sign declaring the patriotism of the shop owner.

          INSERT which READS:
  'We import no British goods
  here. May God favor our cause.'

He watches the milliner show a beautiful roll of silk to a woman of high fashion.

The milliner spots Varick, rolls up the cloth and puts it under the counter.

He whispers to the woman who nods and leaves.

              MILLINER
  How may I serve you, Lieutenant?

              VARICK
  You might tell me if that were a
  roll of silk smuggled from
  London via New York City.

The milliner guages Varick.

He decides that it is no use lying.

              MILLINER
  We do no real harm. Every one of
  fashion wants it, the men as
  well as the ladies. And we only
  use Patriot teamsters to haul
  it in. I could make you a nice
  shirt.

A Screenplay

                    VARICK
I need a nice shirt to testify before Congress but I will feel more honest in homespun. Good day, Sir.

Varick leaves and does not shut the door behind him.

The milliner follows him to the door and hisses fiercely.

                    MILLINER
Do you think trade will stop because of... words on paper. Ask your little puffed-up Congressmen where their fancy clothes originate. How simple can you be!

MATCH DISSOLVE TO:

INT. TEMPORARY YORK CONGRESSIONAL MEETING ROOM - MORNING

Benedict Arnold is pacing and speechifying in the long, narrow room.

John Hancock is playing with a pen at his desk.

Other members of the court martial board are glassy-eyed or stirring slowly, trying to stay awake.

In the audience near Hancock, Samuel Adams is scribbling notes.

Sitting next to him Joseph Reed is

fidgeting and fuming.

> ARNOLD
> ...Can any matter supercede that of honor? If any of these charges has merit, the blood I have spent in defense of my country will be insufficient to obliterate the stain. A man's reputation is sacrosanct and must be kept inviolate. To be escorted here under guard when one has repeatedly pleaded for a court martial to clear one's name? Is it not nobler to resign one's commission with honor intact than to serve under a false cloud of suspicion. If I have erred it is in my zeal to conduct my country's business as if the perilous survival of our cause –

Reed stands for recognition. Hancock grants it immediately.

REED General Arnold.

> ARNOLD
> -- urged speed and decision on us all.

> REED
> It seems, General Arnold, that you are willing to admit the possibility of your having made a mistake, but the way you humbly phrase it, it seems more likely that the Good God

A Screenplay

>   Almighty might make a mistake
>   before you should.

Arnold seems lost in thought. He does not look directly at Reed.

>   ARNOLD
>   I do not choose to denigrate
>   religion by casting
>   aspersions on The Almighty.
>   A man's religious beliefs are as
>   sacrosanct as a man's
>   reputation. Many a dark night
>   my soul has been sustained by
>   my faith in Providence – those
>   especially dark nights when men
>   with resources hold their purse
>   strings as though they would
>   damn the world rather than part
>   with a dollar to their army.
>   was it not God who helped us
>   liberate Fort Stanwix from the
>   forces of darkness? These *are*
>   the times that try men's souls
>   -- when belief in...

Samuel Adams leans toward Reed and whispers.

>   SAMUEL ADAMS
>   Marvelous, Reed! You've given
>   him enough ammunition to fire
>   away for another hour.

Arnold has turned away from Reed who sits down.

>   ARNOLD
>   ...there have been dark days

when I have been ashamed of being born in America -when there is no answer to the questions why they who have the choice choose not to reinforce our army nor feed nor clothe nor pay them, days when only The Almighty...

              REED
If I had a musket handy, I would shoot him now.

MATCH DISSOLVE TO: EXT. TRAIL LEADING TO FARMHOUSE - NIGHT

Varick rides sleepily along the trail until he comes closer to a farmhouse.

He sees cracks of light behind the heavy curtains and hears music.

Varick opens the gate and closes it behind him.

He calls when he is within fifty yards of the house.

             VARICK
Hale the house!

The music stops immediately and most of the light disappears.

             VARICK
I am Richard Varick -- a patriot from Reverend McCrae's house in the Valley. Is there a welcome here for a weary lieutenant of

A Screenplay

the Continental Army?

Silence prevails.

Slowly a musket is eased through a slit near the main window.

> FARMER
> Who comes with you?

> VARICK
> I am alone... en route to York, Pennsylvania per ord -- to wait upon General Arnold.

> FARMER
> Come slowly in. Leave your weapons without.

Varick pats his musket in its saddlecase and makes a show of hanging his sword and tying his pistol to the saddle horn.

Two young men with muskets run from the house and cover each other as they check to the trail beyond the gate.

Varick enters the house and finds the farmer and his wife sitting in rocking chairs by one candle in the parlor.

> VARICK
> I saw no green on your fences or your door. You are good Whigs? Not Tories?

> FARMER
> Not Whigs. Not Tories. We are good farmers tilling God's

earth.

                VARICK
    God save you then.

A charged silence ensues.

Varick hears a noise from another room. He strains to see.

                FARMER
    What is Mrs. McCrae's maiden name?

               VARICK
    Ahh -- I think it O'Brien. She mentions it rarely.

The farmer leaps from his chair and claps his hands.

                FARMER
    All right then! Bring John Walter Charles forth!

Varick is startled as candles and lanterns are lit by more than a dozen people who charge smiling and talking into the parlour from inner rooms.

A young woman carries an infant who wakes up and cries.

An older woman carries an enormous ham and an older man a huge turkey.

The table is moved and filled with platters of food.

A Screenplay

> FARMER
> A christening celebration Lieutenant Varick.

> VARICK
> Con -- gratulations. Are you -- hiding--from someone?

> FARMER
> Anyone who wants what we have.

> VARICK
> Have you no interest in escaping the tyranny of England?

> FARMER
> We surely do -- while you are here. when the Tories come we will curse you rebels. All the same we will get up before dawn and work our fields and care for our stock.

> VARICK
> Is that all?

> FARMER
> We now must trust that a young rebel warrior raised in the split home of Jedidiah McCrae will keep a discreet tongue.

> VARICK
> Oh -- I would never -- you can trust –

The farmer's wife stuffs a deviled egg in Varick's mouth. She pulls him to a cleared space and begins dancing. Varick tries to smile and dance and not choke.

MATCH DISSOLVE TO:

INT. UPSTAIRS LOBBY YORK BUILDING - DAY

Small groups of men and a few ladies are buzzing about the court martial.

In a far corner Arnold is surrounded by young officers.

Samuel Adams hears snatches of conversation -- 'Resignation would be deadly... He means it... Gates is a pillow, Arnold a rock' -- before he joins Joseph Reed and John Hancock.

>SAMUEL ADAMS
>If Arnold resigns half the militia leave and the British will slice through Gates like a stuffed goose. New York is lost and Our United American States states cut in half. We must keep him active in the northern department.

>REED
>I will agree to one thousand pounds and a gift horse because of Stanwix, but I will not advance him in seniority above the others and -

>SAMUEL ADAMS
>And?

A Screenplay

> REED
> ...and he will need to prove every haypenny above the thousand to my council's satisfaction. We know this fox. Should John Burgoyne or Sir William Howe take my wife prisoner I will do no more for Benedict Arnold -- the Fifth or any other.

> SAMUEL ADAMS
> He may not agree to partial measures. Arnold could demand all or nothing. And if it is nothing—

> HANCOCK
> Much as I hate to admit, we should rely on John Adams. His brain is a knotted rope woven into a maze of contradictions. He has the words and ways that will win over our little bantam rooster and keep him fighting in the field. It is our part, if we are not hung, to put up with John's bragging on it for the next fifty or so years. Not a horrible price to pay.

Hancock smiles broadly and turns to include Reed who merely grunts and moves toward the meeting room.

Hancock takes Samuel Adams' arm and they follow.

Betrayal

MATCH DISSOLVE TO:

EXT. ROAD NEAR A VILLAGE - AFTERNOON
(DRIZZLING)

Varick dismounts and checks his horse's shoe.
He leads the horse into the village and to the blacksmith's shop.

The smithy removes the shoe and heats it.

He pours coffee into a mug and adds a slug of rum before handing it to Varick.

> BLACKSMITH
> You are Arnold's man Varick?

> VARICK
> I am Lieutenant Richard Varick assigned to serve with General Benedict Arnold, a true Patriot. I am no one's man but my own.

> BLACKSMITH
> Yes, yes. We are all going to be free and independent and suck on the tit of happiness. I will not need to build fires in the early morning dark.

> VARICK
> We are not promising heaven. We will all work but we will be working to strengthen our own nation, not the corruption that is called England.

A Screenplay

           BLACKSMITH
And how long until we poison our new state? Breed our own corruption?

           VARICK
Don't you wish to rule your own affairs? Carve out your own destiny?

The blacksmith does not respond. Instead, he pounds fiercely on the horseshoe.

           VARICK
Is there a good inn nearby?

           BLACKSMITH
The William Pitt Tavern. Not directly in your way but worth the few miles. Not as brim full of Tories and trimmers.

           VARICK
I know the place.

           BLACKSMITH
Dirty inns around here full of cutthroats ready to shed blood for a few shillings. And turn coat for a haypenny. Ignore the Pitt Tavern loafers. They talk a mighty game -- independence -- freedom. Let them work a hearth for a day. Sweat the silliness out of them.

           VARICK
You seem an honest man. Are you

not... stirred by the chance to -

                    BLACKSMITH
Have another rum coffee. I am...
happy for those who find King
George and Parliament
oppressive... but... I much
prefer a tax collector sitting
fat and groggy in a London
coffee house than one living
next door and poking about my
premises. And what is to keep
Washington from becoming a sad
sorry version of a king? Can you
guarantee me that he won't sieze
government?

                    VARICK
General Washington would never -
- George Washington is a a Free
Mason and a Patriot!

                    BLACKSMITH
And I am a Presbyterian and a
blacksmith. Does any of that
matter if I decide to cheat my
custom? How much harder for a
man to resist the trappings and
temptations of power when all
about you...

INT. WILLIAM PITT TAVERN - EVENING

Varick is drinking and trying to engage the
innkeeper who is talking at the far end of
the bar, or anyone, in conversation.

He is ignored until Alinda Breitvogel

comes downstairs in a large loose low-cut dress.

                    VARICK
          Every -- every officer in this
          and every army is supposed to
          make money from his commission.
          It's the rule. Arnold isn't any
          more guilty -- except for the
          mad schemes and the fierce lies
          -- than the rest of them. Is he?
          Think on it. He gave them
          receipts for Quebec down to the
          haypenny and they argued
          them now for near -- now --
          two years. wouldn't you hide
          your Valcour receipts and say
          they were burned in battle?
          (slams his tankard on the bar)
          Wouldn't you!

                    INNKEEPER
          Put your money on the bar if you
          want another dram. I remember
          you -- one of Arnold's men.
          Another slow payer.

                    VARICK
          Well... yes. But not his toady.
          I do not false -- I won't fawse
          —

Alinda comes up behind Varick.

                    ALINDA
          Falsify. My Mohawk Valley
          lieutenant will not falsify --
          what? His fascination with my
          chest?

Betrayal

> VARICK
> Bright Bird! I mean -- Alinda. They are -- you are -- beautiful. What are you doing -

> ALINDA
> I work here. Mostly above stairs.

Varick frowns.

> ALINDA
> It's some better than seven years in slavery eating slops while the family wears London silks and the husband bellows for me after tavern -- but where is my gallant lieutenant headed?

> VARICK
> You left so quickly.

> ALINDA
> Twas time. When Our Little General slips into his genius of war costume he has no time for sport.

> VARICK
> General Arnold asks me to testify at his court martial in York where Congress has run to. He calls my testimony for General Schuyler 'generous.' What do you think that means, Alinda?

A Screenplay

>   ALINDA
> It means he thinks you stretched
> the truth to save Schuyler's
> skin. It means he expects
> you'll do the same for him.

>   VARICK
> I don't lie. I don't intend to
> lie. I will tell the truth as
> I know it I feel it... we need
> him - Alinda I -I used my
> intended's death -- Burt's
> intended -- to -

>   ALINDA
> To get these fat oafs off
> their asses. Did you have to
> show them which end of a musket
> to point at the enemy.? I heard
> something of Jane McCrea --
> raped in her own farmyard?

>   VARICK
> No! The truth is -

Alinda begins to massage Varick's neck and shoulders.

>   ALINDA
> And the truth is?

>   VARICK
> She was lately Burt's fiancee --
> on her way to join him with
> Burgoyne... Arnold is not a
> saint but not the blackest
> sinner either. Jenny loved me --
> He sells passes. He invests in
> -- enterprises. He is on the

lookout to earn large sums of money -- but aren't they all? She's gone now. I never said goodbye... Only Arnold may be hungrier and less careful in disguising his -

                    ALINDA
A thousand times more so and subtle as a cannon. But always shocked to find he has shot himself in the foot. When are you due in York?
Varick fumbles a letter out of his vest pocket.

                    VARICK
Ahhh -- a few days ago --
(reads) no -maybe a week ago -

                    ALINDA
What is keeping you -- have you drunk up your trip money?

Varick fumbles in his pocket. He takes out two bags which are both more than half full.

                    VARICK
Not yet. I am asked -- asked also by Sergeant Sul a sergeant to testify on behalf of those who would seek to call General Arnold to task for his -- errors.

                    ALINDA
Who seek to crucify him.

A Screenplay

> VARICK
> They think I know a few damning facts that —

> ALINDA
> Do you?

> VARICK
> I —— he may have —— privy to—

> ALINDA
> It's all right Richard Varick. I shall not besiege you. It seems you have a civil war raging yet inside. We'll have a drink and see what needs doing to get you a good night's sleep.

Alinda signals to the innkeeper.

INT. BEDROOM OF WILLIAM PITT INN – NIGHT

Alinda steers an unsteady Varick toward the bed.

She begins undressing him and herself as he clings to the bedpost with one hand and holds his journal in the other.

> VARICK
> I think I love you.

> ALINDA
> If it keeps you at attention —— all right.

> VARICK
> If it keeps me —— you're with

child!

> ALINDA
> I can't talk and attend to the business of a French kiss at the same moment.

> VARICK
> Business? A French kiss?

> ALINDA
> Good choice. Sit on the bed. You look like a toppler. Do you intend to clutch that book throughout the night.

Varick looks at the journal as if discovering a strange object in his hand.

> VARICK
> I don't think I need this. Would you burn it for me?

> ALINDA
> In due time my gallant warrior. We'll damp this other fire first.

CUT TO:

EXT. BURGOYNE'S CAMP - NIGHT

General Burgoyne and his mistress are dancing wildly around a huge fire where the remains of a roasted lamb are on a spit.

Colonel Baum's wife watches disapprovingly. Her children are fussy

A Screenplay

and sleepy. She holds the youngest girl in her arms.

A Hessian soldier without a pack or helmet dismounts on the edge of the circle and delivers a letter to Walter who demands it and brings it to Phillips.

He sips a drink, unfolds the letter, and stands up quickly as he reads.

Officers and their ladies dance moderately or whisper and smile.

Redcoat and Hessian soldiers and a few Tories watch from a distance.

A soldier and his woman on a nearby hill slip into the night. Walter stands by.

The music stops.

Burgoyne and his mistress dance for several seconds before realizing that there is no more music.

> BURGOYNE
> Play on!

The lead musician looks for help to Colonel Phillips.

> PHILLIPS
> You've given the order, General, for an early march.

> BURGOYNE
> What's that got to do with music! Play on! I've never

missed a morning muster yet Phillips.

     MISTRESS
 (giggles) Nor an evening one, Johnny.

The musicians wearily pick up their instruments.

Burgoyne touches his mistress's bare shoulder and starts rubbing downward. She stops his hand gently when it touches her breast.

All turn on hearing the hoofbeats of two riders and the shouted answer to a sentry's challenge.

    SERGEANT BURBANK
 Albany by God and King George!

Sergeant Burbank and the Tory Rider rein their horses just short of the fire circle.

Burbank leaps down and runs to Colonel Phillips who returns his salute.

Burgoyne joins them.

    SERGEANT BURBANK
 I come from Fort Stanwix. We are finished there. Colonel St. Leger is limping back to Canada. The Indians have turned on us. They run before Arnold and Morgan.

A Screenplay

              PHILLIPS
Arnold! We are told he has nothing but a few hundred sorry militia.

         SERGEANT BURBANK
The halfwit Yost brought word he has a few thousand and Morgan's riflemen. This Tory rider –

           BURGOYNE
Loyalist, Sergeant. A larger term for an esteemed ally.

         SERGEANT BURBANK
(saluting) Sir! He brings word that Sir William Howe has sailed for Philadelphia. This frees Washington to send Continentals and –

            PHILLIPS
His Excellency knows the ramifications, Sergeant. Thank you. (to Tory Rider) And you. Take care of your horses and refresh yourselves. Walter!

             WALTER
Colonel! (takes reins) You poor lads will have to make do with lamb and champagne. Your everyday fare, eh?

Walter grins at his witticism.

Sergeant Burbank and the Tory rider exchange a puzzled look as they follow him.

Betrayal

>   BURGOYNE
> We'll stop now.

The musicians pack up.

The officers and their ladies bow their goodnights.

>   MISTRESS
> Coming, Johnny?

>   BURGOYNE
> But a while. I'll wait for
> Colonel Phillips.

His mistress blows Burgoyne a kiss and moves unsteadily toward their tent.

>   PHILLIPS
> For me, Sir?

>   BURGOYNE
> To share the news from
> Bennington. That is the message
> you received, n'est ce pas?

>   PHILLIPS
> I did not think you would wish
> to sour the gaiety.

>   BURGOYNE
> Fortunes of war.

>   PHILLIPS
> From a junior officer: (reads)
> 'An unmitigated disaster...

EXT. HESSIAN CAMP AT BENNINGTON - DAY

A Screenplay

We HEAR Phillips reading the officer's letter.

We SEE hordes of men reporting to Skene, taking loyalty oaths to the King, fixing white pieces of paper to their hats, casually taking positions at the rear of the Hessians.

                    PHILLIPS
    (V.O.) 'Ugly men drifted into
    our camp. We few British
    officers warned Skene that they
    were suspicious but he would
    have none of it. This was the
    outpouring of Loyalists he had
    been awaiting. He gave them sign
    and countersign, had them affix
    white paper to their hats so
    the savages would not shoot
    them if the rebels attacked
    and, incredibly, let them go
    where they would. They formed
    loosely to our rear. The rebels
    under John Stark attacked.

We SEE rebel militia dressed the same as the professed Loyalists attack the Hessians and Indians from the front.

The professed Loyalists reveal their true allegiance by firing from the rear, catching the Hessians and Indians in a crossfire.

Confused, the Indians slip away.

Philip Skene takes a horse and gallops off. Colonel Baum is killed.

Betrayal

The Hessians scatter.

They are run down and killed or captured. One is slain after he tries to surrender.

> PHILLIPS
> (V.O.) 'We were caught in murderous crossfire. The Indians did not know whom to shoot. They and Philip Skene disappeared. Nine hundred or more slain, wounded, captured, missing. Baum is dead. For God's sakes, send a relief column to bring the survivors in.'

BACK TO SCENE

> BURGOYNE
> And you await my orders to act?

> PHILLIPS
> No, Sir. When we had not heard from Baum by yesterday, I sent five hundred regulars in relief.

> BURGOYNE
> Good man!

> PHILLIPS
> I ordered the relief column to send couriers twice daily. None have arrived and I fear the worst... John, we could return to Quebec and await reinforcements for the spring.

> BURGOYNE
> And let this rabble boast they

> have driven His Majesty's troops
> back to Canada two seasons in a
> row. Arnold crowing and Gates
> writing to Walpole. I'd be the
> laughing stock of Parliament --
> all of London. And... I have my
> definite orders. No, William.
> This army must not retreat.

Burgoyne takes the letter from Phillips.
He reads it as he walks away slowly past
the bright banners decorating the dancing
ground.
A patrol returns to the lines.
The patrol leader wearily speaks the
password of the day.

> PATROL LEADER
> Albany by God and King George.

CUT TO:

INT./EXT. THE WILLIAM PITT TAVERN - DAY

Alinda is massaging the shoulders and neck
of a huge filthy teamster and talking over
her shoulder to Varick.

He tries to glare at her through the cloud
of a hangover.

> ALINDA
> Don't pout Richard Varick. We
> had a good tumble and we are
> free of owing. Why expect more?
> Or did you think we were
> engaged?

Betrayal

            VARICK
  Is that all that that means to—

Varick and Alinda are distracted by noise outside as two horsemen gallop into the innyard.

            ARNOLD
  Hale the inn!

            ALINDA
  It's The General!

Alinda rushes out to greet Arnold who is putting a tall caparisoned horse through his paces around and around the innyard to the amusement of Sullivan.

Varick follows tentatively.

The innkeeper frantically searches through his dusty shelf of bills.

            ARNOLD
  Young Missy! I should take time to renew our friendship but I have promises to keep. After we thrash John Burgoyne, I'll find you here and -- is that Lieutenant Richard Varick skulking about. What have you been up to?

Arnold's attention is drawn to Alinda who is posing and preening and grinning.

            ARNOLD
  Of course! This is why you are late to my court martial.

A Screenplay

VARICK
I had to take care of -- my brother -special care.

ARNOLD
Yesss? No matter. Congress has awarded me this magnificent brute and a thousand pounds for the relief of Fort Stanwix. It is only a matter of time before they establish me in my correct rank of senior major general and reimburse all the debts I have incurred in the service of my country. I am assured, practically guaranteed, this by John Adams and other political gentlemen. And Joseph Reed is choking on sour apples.

VARICK
Congratulations then, General Arnold.

ALINDA
Time for one ale to celebrate?

INNKEEPER
Who pays these bills?

Arnold takes out his wallet and hands money to the innkeeper who enthusiastically counts it and then shows disappointment.

ARNOLD
More to come. Add ten pounds for your patience and I will settle all as soon as Arnold looks down

at Alinda who has her hand on
his calf rubbing his new silk
stocking.

           ARNOLD
Dearly would I love to celebrate
with you Missy but we have
Gentleman Johnny in a box and
Sir William Howe, instead of
sailing north, has gone for
glory and ease to
Philadelphia. Burgoyne will
get no help there. (to Varick)
Come to Saratoga and we will run
the Redcoats and Indians and
Tory scum to hell or London.

           VARICK
My brother needs –

           ARNOLD
Are we not all your
brothers. Your country needs
you. Come to Saratoga,
Lieutenant -- no! Captain
Varick. Come to Saratoga where
your new commission awaits you
and we will set a hard
tune for Johnny Burgoyne to
dance. On, King Louis! On!

Arnold draws his sword, spurs his horse,
and charges off in a cloud of dust.

Alinda runs after, laughing and tossing
pebbles.

Varick runs a few steps, tries to think

of something to say, and stops.

Sullivan trots by.

                SULLIVAN
    I never said he was a dullard.

He spurs his horse to a gallop and disappears into a cloud of dust with both thumbs raised.

                SULLIVAN
    Up the Republic! Erin go bragh!

                              CUT TO:

EXT. MCCRAE FARM - EVENING

Varick and Burt are talking.

Burt is seated and calm wrapped in a blanket.

Varick is agitated and pacing much as Arnold paces.

In the background Lottie Smith is changing the bandage on Joseph's calf and talking non-stop.

Reverend McCrae is reading the Bible to Arthur who is wolfing down food served by Mrs. McCrae and occasionally nodding in Reverend McCrae's direction.

                VARICK
    I won't leave you, Burt, ever.

Varick pulls Burt's blanket higher,

Betrayal

cutting off his view. Burt pushes it down.

> BURT
> That's the most frightening statement I have heard, Richard -- ev -- ever!

> VARICK
> I am not going back into service. I must take care of my brother. I am sick of sunshine patriots. Everyone feathering his own nest. I have done enough for my country.

> BURT
> Who calls enough? A soldier comes bl -bleeding to our Thomas. Does he dress the wound or tuh -- tell it it has bled enough?

Alinda comes from the house.

Varick shakes his head as if to rid it of the question.

> BURT
> When Alinda has labor can she call--

> VARICK
> Enough! I call enough. Please Burt. I have done my share. I must nurse you back to health. To you I owe my first allegiance. And Reverend McCrae. You are my bother -- brother. Joseph too.

A Screenplay

          BURT
I am. Both. Mother McCrae and Alinda and Lottie will nurse Father and me and Joseph. And we will help Alinda in her time of confinement. We are through with our war, but you are not with yours. We understand that you must act on your principles.

Varick has a faraway look as he fumbles with Burt's blanket.

          VARICK
My principles.

Alinda reaches as if to massage Burt's neck but stops and intertwines her fingers.

          BURT
As much as you are not a farmer Richard, you are ten times more not a nurse.

          ALINDA
Teach Our Little General subtle Richard Varick. Bring him through safely and you with him. Come home to see your neph -my child.

          VARICK
I am not going.

          BURT
Yes, Richard. Tell me about the new corn ss -- seed we are trying in the far acres and what you will contribute to this

experiment.

Varick looks pained.

                VARICK
I -- am -- not.
Alinda turns away slightly to hide a smile.

                ALINDA
  When you are firm, Richard, you
  are most impressive.

                VARICK
  I am not going to Saratoga.

FADE OUT MONTAGE:

Militia rushing to Saratoga.

Gates sipping tea and scrutinizing maps.

His aides packing horses.

Arnold on horseback leading a charge on a British redoubt.

Morgan directing his men up trees to shoot British and Hessian officers.

Piggott preparing rope snares.
Indians slipping into the woods. John Burgoyne rallying his troops.

Arnold shot in leg, falls, sits up, shoots The Young Private who is poised with bayonet above Arnold but hesitates.

A Screenplay

Morgan protects Arnold from others.

Varick and Sullivan drag Arnold from danger.

Principal with the British and Second Runner with the Americans come face to face, hesitate, and then raise their tomahawks simultaneously to attack each other.

Varick shoots and wounds Sergeant Burbank who has crawled up into firing position.

EPILOGUE ROLLS

British and Hessian ranks break and run.

Piggott and Sullivan and Morgan's men pick off the soldiers running from the battlefield.

The Young Private staggers into one of Piggott's snares.

EPILOGUE

Richard Varick and thousands of minute men from New York and New England did go to Saratoga in the fall of 1777 to answer the call of glory or duty.

They shocked the world by defeating Burgoyne's army.

Soon after France joined America in

Betrayal

openly warring on England.

Three years later a disgusted and financially desperate Benedict Arnold picked the wrong side and -- claiming noble motives of enlightened patriotism and a hatred of 'the Popish French'-- defected to the British.

Other than George Washington, the American most stunned by this treason was Arnold's valued but uninformed aide, Colonel Richard Varick.

Humpty Dumpty Sat on a wall Humpty Dumpty Had a great fall.
All the King's horses
And all the King's men
Could not put Humpty Dumpty
Together again...

FADE OUT

THE END

www.ingramcontent.com/pod-product-compliance
Lightning Source LLC
Chambersburg PA
CBHW022100090426
42743CB00008B/659